7/7/94

979.494
A

Alan-Williams,
Gregory.

C. 1

A gathering of
heroes.

A GATHERING OF HEROES

A GATHERING OF HEROES

Reflections on Rage and Responsibility

A Memoir of the Los Angeles Riots

Gregory Alan-Williams

ACADEMY CHICAGO PUBLISHERS

3 4873 00108 6917

Published in 1994 by
Academy Chicago Publishers
363 West Erie Street
Chicago, Illinois 60610

Library of Congress Cataloging-in-Publication Data

Alan-Williams, Gregory.
    A gathering of heroes : reflections on rage and
responsibility : a memoir of the Los Angeles riots /
Gregory Alan-Williams.
        p.   cm.
    ISBN 0-89733-404-3 : $18.95
    1. Riots—California—Los Angeles—History—
20th century. 2. Violence—California—Los Angeles—History—20th Century. 3. Los Angeles
(Calif.)—Race relations. 4. Racism—California—
Los Angeles. 5. Alan-Williams, Gregory. I. Title.
F869.L89N4   1994   93-44273
979.4'94053—dc20   CIP

For
Harry & Chuck
and
Mrs Nellie Travis-Boyd

I am grateful to all of those who gathered for me as I endeavored to sort and to share my thoughts. Aaron Darsas, thanks for your insight and encouragement. And thanks to Jan Darsas for being in Salem and introducing me to Facing History. Bill Geller, what would I do without your reality-based critique and wisdom? Julie Shannon, your music has given you immortality. Debbie Notkin, editor of my original manuscript, thanks for quietly invoking the rules of good grammar and making me dig deeper. Betty Husted, I will always treasure your wonderful early artwork. Ms Mims, Ms Muse, Ms Cooper what would I do without ya'll. Special thanks to Elie Wiesel for writing *Night*. A thousand thanks and bravos! to Anita Miller, my editor, and all the good folks at Academy for such a warm and rewarding collaboration.

God bless you, Georgia, for making me write so long ago.

James Sanders, I miss you. And I'll see you when I get there.

CONTENTS

Map and photographs on pages 103-112

PREFACE

Since that first fateful day of the Los Angeles riots, media people, friends and folks on the street have asked me why I chose to risk my own safety to come to the aid of a stranger. The more I responded to this question the more I consciously understood that I am not a man of my own making, that "the content of my character" was formed by my struggle with life and by the wisdom and sacrifices of many people who throughout the years have intervened on my behalf in that struggle. The wonderful truth I have discovered is that on Wednesday, April 29, 1992, the best and the worst of these synthesized to a single purpose: the preservation of a human life.

It is said that we are primarily products of our environment. And that the preservation of life at the risk of one's own is the greatest possible demonstration of love. If these things are true, then the willingness and the ability to help Takao Hirata at that crucial moment in both our lives must have come from the collective energies both of the many who have given me love, and of those who have given me only hate.

Over the past months, I have tried to retrace the path that led me that day to the intersection of Florence and Normandie avenues. I have endeavored to identify some of the personalities and experiences that helped prepare me for what may well have been a summit of my destiny. For just as the journey to that summit did not begin on Wednesday, April 29th, 1992, neither was I alone on that corner. I was surrounded by people from my past. Voices of courage and compassion, urging me to act, telling me how to move, and some warning me not to move at all—that it was not my place.

I am writing this to share with you the identity of that day's true heroes. Heroes whose hearts and minds reached out through me to rescue a fellow human being.

Just as significant, however, are the

descriptions of those whose displays of bigotry and hatred have enabled me to see the true nature of the beast of intolerance that would destroy us all.

Perhaps the wonderful irony is that those who tried to extinguish in me the spirit of love and brotherhood ultimately helped kindle the flame.

Throughout the years many heroes, male and female, have passed my way—considerably more than are mentioned in these pages. To my knowledge, none of them ever rushed into a burning building or dragged a victim from a mob. Their courage was of another kind, steady and constant. Most heroism is like that. The true heroes are those who do the best they can on behalf of themselves and others. Folks who go to work every day, despite the drudgery, then come home and love a bunch of crazy kids who don't really appreciate them.

Every day, around the world, heroes feed the hungry, house the homeless, clothe the naked, and teach the so-called hopeless and ignorant. Heroes take the time to share themselves and the wisdom they have gathered on their walk toward destiny. Heroes cry and cry out when there is injustice, regardless of their ties to the unjust.

My good deed made the headlines, and so my actions may seem special or unique, but each day, from sunrise to sundown, somewhere, heroism is manifest as simply as "Each one, teach one. . . A fed one, feed one. . . A saved one, save one."

Where does hate begin?
How does it grow?
Who plows the field
And then returns to sow?
Who plants the seed
And keeps hate alive?
In a world that longs for peace,
How does hate survive?

JULIE SHANNON
FROM THE SONG "ONE BREATH"

1.
CRIMES OF THE HEART

I laughed when I heard the verdict in the Rodney King beating trial. It was reflex. My father figure, Mr Bus, used to laugh whenever he was temporarily deprived of his dignity by the words or deeds of white folks; laughter took the edge off.

Mr Bus would tap a red-and-white pack of Winstons against a bony forefinger, grip the furthest filter with his lips, then roll a flat wide thumb across the lighter he had pulled from the pocket of his paint-speckled coveralls. He'd close one eye, throw his head back and inhale deeply. For a moment he wouldn't breathe, he would just watch the sky. As he lowered his head toward his Stacey Adams dress shoes, decorated with a thousand droplets of interior latex and washable oil-based semi-gloss, I would catch a glimpse of a smile. Then, only the top of his flattop haircut would be visible, as he slowly shook his head and released a nasal snicker along with the poisonous grey smoke that soothed him.

The jury's decision reached me via my car radio at about 3:50 p.m., as I cruised down Century Boulevard on my way to the gym. I was still chuckling to myself when I walked into the Family Fitness Center in the basement of the Airport Hilton Hotel. As I passed the wall-mounted TV and its few viewers hurriedly pumping away on Lifecycles and Stairmasters, I slowed and looked back over my shoulder to catch their reactions to the news anchor's somber analysis of the verdict. For a few seconds my eyes panned back and forth between the audience and the screen. I grinned and let out a laugh, but there was no break in their rhythm, no change of focus.

I was hoping for someone to laugh with. Someone to join me in a chorus of an old "Ain't that a bitch," kind of laugh. The kind that comes when an old ache you thought was gone starts hurting again. A trio would have been nice, but a duet would do, just so I wouldn't feel like I was hurting alone after such a long time.

Actually, it hadn't really been that long. Just a year earlier, I had watched video-taped footage of an unarmed man on his knees being beaten by a mob of peace officers. I laughed then too, after seeing it a dozen times; it took the edge off.

Disappointed and feeling just a little bit foolish, I turned and headed for the aerobics room up the hall. Several people were already there, sitting, stretching, silently waiting for class to begin. Not wanting to risk looking stupid again, I kept a straight face and chuckled solo in my head. I was trying to keep from talking to myself about the verdict or maybe I was trying not to listen to myself talk about it; whichever, something had to give. Laughter only worked for so long—just long enough to ease the hurt. In time, when pain began to fade, anger would take its instinctual place; then rage, as anger's heir, would slowly begin its rise to self-destruction.

I was about eight years old when anger

and I first became friends; anger comforted me in a way that tears had ceased to do. It was probably about this same time that, along with life's standard issue of slings and arrows, I began to be confronted with the harsh realities of racism.

One of my earliest recollections concerns a second-grade teacher who banked her spare change in little 35 mm film canisters. The tiny depositories were secured in an unlocked vault which also served as a storage closet for paste, construction paper, and other classroom supplies. Wouldn't you know it, one day several of the canisters turned up missing.

"Who took the money?" she asked her class of seven-year-olds.

Being a clownish kid, I stood, placed my hand over my heart and, à la George Washington, announced, "I cannot tell a lie, teacher, I stole the money!" Of course I was joking, but when my teacher bit the corner of her lower lip and called me a "thieving nigger," I knew she had accepted the admission of guilt as genuine. As she approached my desk, beet-red and ranting,

I explained that I hadn't really taken the money. "I was just trying to be funny," I told her.

The teacher ignored my pleas of innocence and insisted that I was the "dirty little nigger" who had done the deed. She continued toward me and I bolted for the door. Blocking my way, she ordered me to be still. Scared to death, I started scurrying around the room like a rat looking for a place to hide. My classmates jumped out of the way, recoiling from me as if a touch would make them thieving little niggers too. Their reactions and my pitiful pleadings made me ashamed of myself. I was bawling and begging, "No, teacher! No, teacher! I didn't take it, teacher! I didn't!"

The room was in chaos and I was cornered. Her fists were clenched and I knew she was going to hit me. In a panic, I shoved a desk toward her, trying to delay her advance and clear a path of escape. The desk struck her solidly on the legs; she stumbled. The other children screamed and broke for the door. I followed close behind, well aware that I was doomed. As I ran down the hall, I felt an almost indescribable horror—

I had hit a teacher; only Jesus knew what would happen to me now.

Terror-stricken, I wandered up and down the school corridors until I was apprehended by the principal, a few student witnesses and a posse of custodians.

At the parent-teacher conference a few days later, my mother steadfastly refused to accept the principal's decision to expel me.

"My son is not violent, and he isn't a thief; and maybe his teacher should consider her choice of words more carefully," she said calmly.

The principal explained that there was no other option. The teacher I had "assaulted" refused to have me in her class. The B-track class was full and the academic work in the A-track class was well beyond my ability; I would only fall miserably behind.

I had been assigned to that C-track classroom a few months earlier after transferring from a predominantly black elementary school. When I enrolled at my new school, I had been placed automatically in the lowest track class.

"Let's try the A class," Mama said, smiling.

The principal consented, but warned that my progress would be closely monitored during a thirty-day academic trial period. I remained in that class for the next four years until I finished the sixth grade.

The feelings of shame, guilt, and worthlessness stayed with me for years after this first experience with overt racism. At the time, however, I didn't view the incident in racial terms. Despite my mother's efforts to explain my teacher's bigotry, I felt that something about me was terribly wrong. In my seven-year-old mind, a teacher, any teacher, was a wonderful divine being. I believed in them as arbiters of who and what was good or bad. "Could someone so right really be so wrong?" I wondered.

Coming of age in a predominantly white, middle-American hometown, I was confronted daily with attitudes and images that nurtured my doubts about my worth. Each evening at our dinner table, Walter Cronkite brought news of my countrymen's often fierce resistance to the concept of my equality. Around seven o'clock, TV's prime time depiction of America at its best combined with the evening news and my daily observations of life in Iowa to leave me with the hidden, destructive suspicion that "colored people" were almost always the exception, rarely the rule.

Over time, I discovered that I could ease the painful impact of those images, and the distress of my personal encounters with bigotry, by erecting barricades of hostility: an angry fortress to conceal shame and sufferings, both real and imagined. By the time I reached high school, I had become a willing prisoner in a secret citadel of rage. My relationships with people became guarded and shallow. I tried to reveal little of my true self or feelings to anyone, white or black. All persons were seen as potential perpetrators of hurt crimes—crimes of the heart. I began to feign indifference and contempt in anticipation of the rejection which I feared would come; do unto others, before they do unto you.

Perhaps the saddest fact of all is that true contempt was reserved almost exclusively for myself: I had contempt for my tragically misperceived failings of ugliness, ignorance, and worthlessness. Safe behind the walls of my fortress, I stared into a mirror of self-hatred, envious and resentful of those so powerful that they could make me despise my own image. Inside my citadel I was shielded to a degree from the forces of hate, but, consequently, I was also cut off from discovery of a wealth of good in myself and the world around me. Although I often succeeded academically and vocationally, my siege mentality made it virtually impossible for me to venture beyond the walls of my safe haven in order to cultivate the life-sustaining fields of trust, friendship, and genuine self-love.

I was unable to grasp the self-defeating nature of my angry isolation, in part, because of an unquestioning belief in the popular rhetoric of the sixties. I believed, as did many others, that rage was my birthright, a legacy of injustice, and a vital requisite to revolution. Sadly, the stamp of conformity meant more to me than the signature of my own experience. For although it was I who most often suffered the day-to-day emotional and psychological consequences of my rage, I clung to the victim-think of the day which supported my delusions that nearly all my demons were born of bigotry. Therefore, responsibility for their exorcism should be laid unreservedly at someone else's door.

Had I realized the ultimate futility of these attitudes, I might have better applied my energies to an absolutely critical challenge which defeated me daily: namely, how to transcend my anger and remain emotionally and psychologically whole in spite of racism, either real or imagined. To become a whole and useful person, I needed first to abandon my no-win, "first strike" response to life. And second, I had to discard the notion that those who had denied my humanity either could or would restore my self-esteem and relieve the trauma that had given rise to my rage.

In 1983 I began to realize that my old friend anger was a liar who had betrayed me. Shortly thereafter, a few new friends with no last names lent me a simple truth. A truth concerning my frantic search for release from the bondage of bigotry and self: "I may not be responsible for the problem," they told me, "but I must be responsible for the solution." My new friends told me that, in order to ascend my walls of rage, I would have to use wings of my own making. Wings constructed of principle, courage and divine grace.

One wintry morning on the south side of Chicago, Nick, an ex-high-roller from Detroit, confronted me with a cup of coffee and a radical idea: "Maybe it's not the world or the people in it that's causin your problem," he said. "Might be the way you're lookin at things."

I thought about his suggestion for a few minutes and quickly decided that Nick was either nuts or an Uncle Tom or both. Despite my skepticism, Nick was patient with me. He recognized his own once-angry image in the numerous masks I wore to hide my pain. After many months and dozens of cups of coffee, Nick persevered to convince me of my individual powerlessness over people, events, and points of view. "You gotta let go of it, or it'll drag ya," he'd say.

As to his view of life's inevitable burdens, Nick explained, "A man can't hardly choose the size or shape of his cross, but a fella's got to work out his own best way of luggin it. If he don't, it'll wear him down, and crush him sure as sugar. But if he learns how to carry it the right way, he might last long enough to figure out how to get the damn thing off his back altogether!"

Then, ever so slowly, Nick's lips would ease into a gold-speckled grin, and we would both laugh loud and long; I, with relief at having found the beginnings of a solution; Nick, because he had learned never to take himself too seriously.

As I sat on the aerobic room floor, on that April day in 1992, with my back, and my heart, against the wall, I thought of Nick and my friends with no last names. Quickly, I went about the crucial business of putting the Simi Valley decision into perspective, a perspective which would not shackle me to the walls of my old shadowy fortress; but one which would leave me free to see the perceived failings of others in the warm light of reason and restraint.

At 4:35 the hip hop music bounded out

of the gym's speaker system. The steady march of the bass line was like a call to arms, a challenge to the enemy within me to a contest of wills.

I enjoy step aerobics because both its beauty and effectiveness lie in the same precision of execution required in the performance of a Marine Corps close-order drill. By graduation day, when the eighty young men of my training platoon floated across the drill field like a single organism, the simultaneous striking of our heels on the deck echoed like the footsteps of a solitary giant. And now, as the aerobics instructor pumped up the volume and speed of the electronic cadence, I marveled again at what seemed like the motion of a single being: forty knees lifting themselves in perfect unison, eighty arms flying up and forward at once, harmoniously reaching for the grail of personal best. Several times I caught glimpses of myself in the mirror, sweaty and strong. The image which kicked and lunged back at me belied the feelings of worthlessness which had surfaced when I learned the jury's decision—a decision I took instantly as a rebuke.

For a few moments, I had slipped back into an old and dangerous frame of mind, a way of looking at the world that imbued the actions and attitudes of others with the power to define my worth. But, by the grace of God, clothed in the wisdom of a few good friends, I had outfoxed that old insanity. The rage which grew to slay me now took flight in the face of a far greater power, a power comprised of spiritual principle, physical certainty and unity of purpose. Amidst the pounding mantra of house music, among that multicultural, bilingual, unisex mass of sweat-soaked humanity, I again saw myself for what I was: a worthwhile human being, who at least for the time being was no longer subject to the misguided opinions of strangers.

Step class ended at exactly 5:30, but I stuck around and took half of the next class too. After working out with a few weights, I headed home. On the way to the elevators I stopped at a pay phone in the hotel lobby to call my wife at work. We talked about what to have for dinner, and I was instructed to pick up coals for the grill and some chicken on the way home. I was about to hang up when I remembered to ask, "Did you hear the verdict?"

"Yeah," Sylest sighed. There was silence. Then, after a moment, she laughed.

. . . I done seen the day many times in my mind.
It's early one morning, and I come bustin through the door...
I say, Mattie, Mattie, wake up! I just seen a blackman,
brownman, whiteman, redman, and yellow man, comin down
the street a callin each other brother!
Wake up woman, it's a brand new day...!
Mine eyes have seen the glory!

FROM *THE LIFE AND TIMES OF DEACON A.L. WILEY*

2.
MY BROTHER'S KEEPER

During the short drive to Ralph's Market at Century and Crenshaw, I listened to radio reports of the violence erupting in South Central Los Angeles. Cars were being pelted with bricks and bottles as they passed through the intersection of Florence and Normandie avenues, and several motorists had been attacked inside their cars. Fresh descriptions of the violence were coming in by the minute. The lead story concerned a white truck driver who had been pulled from his rig and beaten, as dozens of bystanders and several police helicopters looked on, and tens of thousands more watched on their TVs at home.

At Prairie Boulevard, a young white couple pulled to a stop on my left. I glanced at them. The woman returned my look,

smiled sheepishly, then looked away quickly. I wondered if they were listening to the
news, if they knew what was going on just
up the road, and why.

I had an urge to roll down my window
and warn the couple of what might lie
ahead. By the time the light changed I had
decided to mind my own business. I fixed
my gaze straight ahead and drove away, de-
termined to ignore the urge to speak.

I had not spoken to the couple as I
wanted to do because something within
me, something old, frightened and familiar, warned against it. Personally, and politically, I condemned terrorism as an ugly
and dangerous enemy of humanity, yet
even as the conscience of my humanity encouraged me to share my concern, the
voices of a hard heritage pleaded my silence, so that an expression of that concern
would not betray a just and venerable
cause.

Collective experience had taught me
that black folks were generally misjudged
and mistreated equally. Consequently,
I hardly questioned collective wisdom
which dictated that the Black Man's pur-

suit of redress for such mistreatment must be equally monolithic.

In addition, I came of age in the midst of a civil rights consciousness, fundamentally non-violent in nature but with an unfortunate—perhaps necessary—fascist tilt. In my view there was little room in this movement for, or tolerance of, thought or action which might smack of division among the ranks. Rarely were we or our leaders to speak honestly and openly among ourselves, about ourselves; and almost never were we to utter differing views of problems or solutions within earshot of white folks. We were, after all, at war, and loose lips sink ships. It seemed that as we sailed toward the promised land, we would welcome the better of our pale brothers in the bittersweet harmonies of freedom's song, but in our scarred and secret hearts, we would never embrace them as true shipmates.

I realize now that, during the 1960s, the delusion of oneness in all things—experience, hope, and hopelessness—was ingrained in the psyches and "souls" of black folks. For the sake of political necessity, we embraced the racist refrain that we were "all alike." For our enemies, our allies and ourselves, that refrain fueled an illusion of perfect unity: one for all, and all for one, personally or collectively; come hell or high water.

So, as a very real product of that illusion, I turned away from the couple beside me, betraying the God consciousness within me, unquestioningly adhering to an oppressed and brutalized people's code of fearful silence.

That couple stayed on my mind as I pulled into the grocery store parking lot. I parked, turned the radio down a tad, and thought. I thought about the course many unsuspecting people were taking toward the intersection of Florence and Normandie, and about those whose rage might lead them to a disastrous and irreversible destiny. As a former prisoner of rage, I realized that there were others who had not been given the keys to their angry shackles. I grieved for them. I grieved for those on that corner, who were unaware that their willingness to do deliberate harm to another human being was predicated on a tragic and forced devaluation of self. I felt frightened and helpless, in the certainty that many African men and women were unwittingly delivering themselves into the hands of a racist system which revelled at any opportunity to isolate and exterminate them.

A hard-hearted farmer once replied to inquiries about his brother's well-being with the question, "Am I my brother's keeper?" It was a question which had been presented to me many times; first as a child in a Pentecostal congregation, and later as a student of Jesuit scholars. Never before those moments in that grocery store lot, had this question demanded such a sure and immediate answer.

At the age of ten I had stumbled upon the answer to this question, while travelling in the Yucatan peninsula of Mexico. As I came of age in a frightened and selfish society, I simply forgot what that answer was.

The Des Moines YMCA Boys Chorus and Bellringers admitted its first Negro members in 1966. Over the years the chorus of sixty boys, ages ten to eighteen, had earned an international reputation not only for its singing, but for the ringing of over thirty different types of bells. In addition to weekly performances throughout the Midwest, each year the group embarked on a two-week national tour. During my second year as a tenor, we journeyed to the southwest and into Mexico.

The day before a long-awaited shopping spree in Yucatan, our fair-skinned Mexican hosts warned us not to give money to beggars. If we gave to one, they explained, we would be overwhelmed by the multitude of poor people on the street. Taking this as good advice, the group's directors forbade us to share any part of our sixty-dollar spending allowance with the indigenous population.

The next day in the city's open market, I took a break from shopping and stepped onto the street to assay my loot. A small slow clanging turned my attention toward a Mayan woman sitting on the stone walkway, slowly rocking from side to side. With her right hand, she gently waved a battered metal cup. The small brown woman's left arm lovingly cradled a horribly disfigured, palsied child of seven or eight. The child's head was swollen to several times the normal size. His eyes were wide and blank. A small smile grazed his lips. I just stood there and looked at them, shocked by the sudden realization that such helplessness and suffering could really exist. The woman looked into my eyes and raised her cup. I knew which pocket my money was in, but I looked down as I reached inside, not wanting to embarrass her with the tears which were forming thick and heavy in the corner of my eyes. Still trying to avert my gaze, I added several pesos to her cup.

My tears broke free the moment my back was to her. I had been moved in part by pity, but primarily by a similarity of experience. In the helpless posture of that young sick child, I had recognized the familiar life-preserving trust and comfort of a mother's unconditional love.

After taking only a few steps, I turned to take one last look at the two on the sidewalk. The young woman smiled and nodded a small "gracias." Her lips, upturned and pressed gently together, shaped the proud approving smile of my own mother. The look in her loving eyes said that I, not she or her child, had received the greater gift.

That evening I was restricted to my room and given a meal of bread and water for disobeying our directors' instructions and our hosts' sound advice. Later that night, to my eternal gratitude, I was blessed with a taco which my roommate had secured during dinner. In the darkness of our hotel room, I cried again as I envisioned the woman and her son. But I fell into an easy sleep, comforted by a happy feeling that my small gift had somehow touched the very essence of life itself.

In 1986, I visited a poor Catholic parish near the Lake Michigan shore in search of a reconciliation with the faith which I had lost as a young man. During that first visit, I was invited into the rectory kitchen by a young lay worker of Puerto Rican descent, a psychologist recently returned from a lengthy stint in El Salvador. Marco was the most laid-back man of God I had ever met, a real no-pressure preacher. When I explained to him that even though things were going well for me, I still felt empty, Marco just chuckled a little and came back with something like "Yeah, I hate when that happens too."

I expected him to use quotations from the Scriptures to help solve my problem, but Marco talked mostly about rock & roll. After showing me his bass guitar, the psychologist casually mentioned the parish's need of volunteers for its Food Shelf program. Twice a week the church distributed food to the neighborhood's hungry. Marco suggested that the parish would be most grateful if I could make some time in my schedule to come and help out. I was touched by the parish's need, so I figured the least I could do was come back the following Tuesday and lend a hand.

The Food Shelf's coordinator was a middle-aged black man named Clarence, who insisted on overseeing and double-checking every can and commodity that came and went. I was able to accept his way of doing things primarily because of my conversations with Nick. With Nick's help I was coming to believe that even if I did

have all the answers, other folks had a right
to be wrong.

Soon, inventorying the donated food-
stuffs and—most of all—filling and distribut-
ing the bags, became the high points of
my week. Even in the midst of a healthy
acting career and growing self-esteem, I
had never felt more fulfilled and purposeful in all my life than on each Tuesday and
Thursday when I gratefully handed those
groceries to the most cherished of God's
children.

Marco and I talked many times during
my tenure at the Food Shelf and at those
moments when I would try to explain the
joy I experienced as a result of my labor,
he smiled because he already knew—as
the woman in Yucatan had known. I had
come to Marco's parish to find a faith
which I had lost, and a meaning and purpose for living. To this end my friend had
guided me toward the essential first step:
the chance to be reconciled to my brother.

Not long after meeting Marco, I had an
opportunity to hear a bearded, retired
postal worker share his story about a plaque
he had seen somewhere in Kentucky, and

how it had been the signpost he had been seeking in his search for God and himself; the plaque read:

I sought my God, my God eluded me.
I sought my soul, my soul I could not see.
I sought my brothers and sisters,
And I found all three.

I left the parking lot with no illusions of rushing into the fray like Dudley Do-Right, saving the day and reaping the tears and thanks of a grateful victim. I decided to go to the intersection of Florence and Normandie to be my brother's keeper. To try to keep my brother from hurting himself by persuading him not to hurt our brother. To intervene on behalf of those who might have been denied the tools which would have enabled them to navigate their own course toward a kinder and more gentle destiny. With reason and compassion I hoped to illuminate the similarities which bound us all in a common humanity.

I was fully aware that any service I might render at that intersection would not be without compensation; in fact my decision was based largely on self-interest. Perhaps the most important truth I had learned during my time with Nick and his friends was that in order to hold on to principles of personal freedom like justice, charity and mercy (principles which had been so freely given to me) I had to give them away. Merely laying claim to those principles for the sake of their beauty and nobility would only cause them to stagnate within me, and eventually wither and die. Although Nick and others had helped me internalize this truth, it was an impoverished Indian woman and her blind and silent child who first showed me its life-affirming beauty.

"Young man, you've got to stand up for something, or you'll fall for anything."

Mr W.G.
"Evans Avenue"
Southside, Chicago

3.
A PALER VERSION OF MY OWN

Traffic was flowing smoothly as I turned left onto Western Avenue in South Central Los Angeles. On the sidewalk small groups of people, mostly teenagers, were hurrying northward: first walking, then breaking into short runs, slowing again, turning, beckoning impatiently to lagging, laughing friends. All around me were pockets of excited brown-skinned humanity moving toward a promised land of power and retribution just a few blocks ahead, to the north. Most were children, and like children delirious with anticipation, they hurried to claim ringside seats for a macabre carnival at the corner of Florence and Normandie avenues. The "up-to-the-minute," "as-it-happens" news reports on radio and television had promised them thrills, chills and audience participation.

The Simi Valley jury's acquittal of the four Los Angeles Police Department officers charged with the beating of Rodney King had not only stripped African Americans of their dignity and worth, but had diminished the worth of all human beings.   In light of the videotaped evidence of what appeared to be a contemporary enactment of a classic injustice, the white jurors had delivered a clear and painful message not only to African Americans but to the entire world. From outside the courtroom, each finding of innocence seemed to be a declaration that a man of African descent can be savagely beaten in the street while the world watches, and that that beating is not to be considered a crime, but justified, well-deserved, and administered within the boundaries of the law.

The all-white jury was unable to see the forest for the trees—the forest of fear and hatred.   The jury's own fear, their common skin color and culture had blinded them to the ugliness of the crew they had set free, whom they seemed to consider somehow heroic.

And now this carnival of new violence had come to town on the heels of that courtroom circus, which had failed the most expectant and hopeful among its audience. The lady who was flying blind, had missed the trapeze bar during the big finale and fallen to a familiar death under the big top of justice. Ticket holders of color were not surprised by her fall, only hurt and weary after having been taken in again. Many were enraged that they had spent their meager trust on yet another ticket.

A block and a half from Manchester, I spotted a group of teenage boys chasing what appeared to be a young white man down the west side of the street. The man was in full flight, but his pursuers were steadily gaining on him. He looked back over his shoulder, his face twisted with terror; the mob was closing on him. Trying to run faster, he stumbled, losing more ground. The man fled into the lot of a Shell gas station on the corner of Manchester and Western—perhaps seeking safety among its customers. He was nowhere near the pumps when the six assailants felled him with the full force of many blows. He cowered on the ground, under a storm of kicks and punches.

I cut across the oncoming southbound traffic without thinking. The chase I had just witnessed was a familiar scene from my adolescence. I sped into the lot, slammed on my brakes and leaped from the car, yelling, "Leave him alone! Leave him alone!" In all honesty I was screaming at them as much for myself as I was for him.

The speed and intensity of my intrusion caught the young men unawares, and to my surprise and relief, they ran away. Keeping an eye on their retreat, I reached toward the man sitting dazed and confused on the pavement. I looked into his face and saw a paler version of my own. It was clear to me that this was a man of African descent. His skin was fair, almost albino, but his features were deeply and beautifully African.

"What did I do?" he asked.

I pulled him to his feet, laughed and replied, "You didn't do nothin man. You just look kinda white, that's all."

Expecting his assailants to regroup after they realized that they had fled from a nearly middle-aged man with bad knees, I rushed their victim into my car and sped away.

He didn't say a word as I drove him to a safer corner a few blocks away.

"You sure you don't want me to take you home?" I asked.

"Naw, I'm cool," he said softly, looking out the window.

When we reached the corner, he shook my hand and thanked me. I looked away so he wouldn't know that I had seen the tears in his eyes. He got out of the car and walked slowly but steadily to the corner. Physically, he was okay and much too cool to let on that he was hurting on the inside, but I knew. Waiting for the light, he reached deep into his trousers, tucking his shirttail back in its proper place. I imagined that at the same time, he was pushing his pain deeper and deeper inside himself, and at least for the moment, any and all doubts about where and with whom he belonged.

Fear of his pursuers, and the shame of having to run, had twisted the young man's features into a horrified mask the likes of which I had not seen in many years. The mask mirrored the horror I saw on my own

face during childhood nightmares in which
I struggled to escape the contempt of my
peers. In reality their disdain most often
took the form of harmless taunts and laughter. Occasionally there was a fistfight, or
flight from a group of boys through gravel
alleys and fenced backyards to safety behind the wooden front door of my house.
Once inside, fear, shame, and rage would
start to churn painfully in my stomach, and
I would curl into a fetal position on the
bed until I fell asleep. By the time I
awakened to the sound of love calling me
to dinner, and headed to the washroom to
soap my hands and wipe away the signs of
my distress, the uneasy mix within me
had begun to harden like concrete, forming
yet another angry slab on the wall of my
fortress of hatred.

During the second semester of the sev-
enth grade, I tried to abandon that sad
and lonely place in search of some self-
esteem, and something to belong to. I set
my sights on what seemed, from a distance, a
broader and more enlightened landscape.
A region where the quality and earnestness
of my being would not be so cruelly ques-

tioned.

What I failed to realize was, that I was that place and it was me, and where I went, there it would be also.

During my adolescence I was often confronted by "brothers" who doubted the integrity of my ethnicity. I was not labeled an "Uncle Tom" for lack of pigment, but for lack of aptitude on the basketball court and on the concrete playing field under the street lamps, and also, I was told, for "talking funny," too "proper." But in the minds of many of my peers, nothing demonstrated my heart's desire to be white more than the piano practice which took place each day during the neighborhood after-school football and baseball games. Looking back I realize that our athletic ability had become synonymous with our racial identity. We were young men whose self-image was defined, in part, by racist stereotype.

Recently I talked with the mother of an old classmate. Her son, my friend, was imprisoned and had asked his mother to contact me about visiting the institution. The inmates wanted to acknowledge my actions in Los Angeles, and hoped that I would share my experience with several at-risk young people from the surrounding community whom they were trying to help.

During our conversation my schoolmate's mother recalled how years earlier her children had come home perplexed and amused by my seemingly sad detention on the piano bench behind the open screen door. (I often practiced with the front door open in order to keep an eye on the goings-on in the street, and would ease from my classical score into a by-ear rendition of a pop piece when friends passed.) We both laughed at the memory. Then, softly, sadly she muttered something about it all making sense now—that clearly I was the better for it.

Our ensuing silence was filled with thoughts of my friend, her son: strong and dark, muted and nearly invisible behind the walls of a Midwestern state prison. At that moment I didn't feel the better for it at all.

If I was indeed an Uncle Tom and secretly wished to be white, then these

desires plagued me only on weekdays, because every Sunday my mother and I at-
tended the New Jerusalem Church of God
in Christ.   There we sang the congrega-
tional songs we knew by heart, clapped
our hands and beat the tambourine from
the heel of our hands to our elbows as
the choir belted out the music of the Rev-
erend James Cleveland. Mother listened
and fanned herself, while the deacon read
the scripture, concluding with the hope that
the Lord would "Lend a blessing to the
reader and the hearer of his word." I
clutched my seat and breathed in quick
gasps, as the pastor's sermon slowly carried
the church to a roller-coaster-like precipice
of praise. We teetered high atop his words
for what seemed like forever. Then the
organist would strike a piercing high note.
Some woman would scream in holy ecstasy,
no longer able to contain her love for the
Master. Others would start to rock, shiver
and moan.   His divine mission accomplished, head lowered in reverent exhaus-
tion, the sweat-soaked minister appeared
almost to float back to the pulpit in silence. There, without looking, he humbly

accepted the glass of water offered him by
a smiling and satisfied assistant pastor.
The organist, still sustaining the high note
resounding like Gabriel's trumpet, responded
to the water-glass cue by beating out a four-
note bass line on the organ's pedals. A few
feet would start to stomp. The vibration
would spread over the hardwood floor like
gasoline on fire, igniting souls from pew to
pew. The smack and pop of flesh beating
against flesh broke out throughout the
sanctuary, as palms collided in perfect unison on the offbeat. Mama, lifted by the lyrics
in her glad and grateful heart, would rise
smoothly, quickly to her feet and sing, "I
MADE A VOW TO THE LORD!" Several of the
saints, our name for the faithful, would
jump to their feet and exclaim, "AND I WON'T
TAKE IT BACK!"

We were over the top now, pulled by
the weight of our frenzied joy, acceler-
ating toward the final upward rush which
would take us into the arms of God. The
music picked up speed as we flew with
hands and hearts outstretched to Jesus.
Faster and faster, the faithful danced,
swirled, and sang. Just when it seemed that

we had reached the end of our religious thrill ride, the organist would latch on to our spirits with a new chord progression and a few quickly improvised runs on the B-3 with the whirling Leslie speaker. He just wouldn't let us be. So, willingly we went up and away, again, like dark spiritual supermen, saved, sanctified, filled with the Holy Ghost and fire.

For much of my childhood the church was the center of the world and the catalyst of my "colored" community. Our collective wealth, influence and pride were reflected in the sumptuousness of our sanctuaries, the stylishness of the suits we wore to worship, and the shiny newness of the cars parked in the church parking lot. Outside the house of God, a car width from the curb, we were mostly powerless.

Monday through Saturday, attention in my house turned toward another world and dreams of expansion, power and self-determination. The sweet rhythms of James Cleveland were replaced by the rigors of Beethoven and Bach. Brother Dixon's electric guitar licks were softened and modified for the twelve-string acoustic.

The slick vocal riffs I practiced for my solo with the choir were neatly tucked away while Mother and I prepared Broadway standards for Bill Riley's "Talent Search"; the winners got college scholarships and a brand-new shiny red Mustang. I spent many evenings writing orations for the Optimists and the Elks; their winners got scholarships too. In the beginning I adamantly insisted that I could not write an oration, let alone a winning one, but as the date of entry approached, Mother insisted that I could and would. She sat on her stool, while I sat at the kitchen table, my eyes tired from their constant shifting from the page of my text to the thesaurus. I would write a phrase or two, then read it to her. She critiqued, smiling when it worked, advising when it didn't.

Over the years I won a few scholarships, but more importantly I discovered that I could do what I believed I could not do, and what I had been afraid to try.

Weekdays my parent simply tried to help me step just a little further from the curb where sat a "Deuce and a Quarter"—a Buick Electra 225. But on Sunday mornings

she took me back along the path we and
others had made as we laid the track for the
freedom train. We followed the path home,
and lay ourselves down at the bosom of our
mother, the church. We told her of our
trials and our dreams, and in the peace of
her womb we received sustenance and
celebrated the life that was, and the better
life that was to come.

In my small Midwestern community,
the land of hope and opportunity lay
almost exclusively beyond our dark-skinned
sphere of influence. In our isolation, it was
easy to accept the limited images and
stereotypes of ourselves provided by lack
of opportunity and bigotry. Often anything that could be done that "they" had
not told us we should or could do, we
simply didn't do. If anyone did things like
that, there were always some who would
resent it, accusing him of trying to be different or better and turning his back on
the others.

In my adolescent heart of hearts I would
have given anything to be what the fellas
in the neighborhood wanted me to be. But
Mama, who had been born and reared in

the self-reliant reality of rural Mississippi, realized that as African-American kids, we were blinded to our own potential by our youth, bigotry, low self-esteem and the self-pitying rhetoric of our time. In a constant, devoted attempt to save me from my enemies and from myself, she pushed and prodded me toward the peak of my potential despite my own willingness to accept the mark of mediocrity promoted by some and unwittingly acquiesced to by others.

As I watched the fair-skinned young black man cross the street, I prayed that God would bless him, as He had blessed me, with heroes and sheroes to rescue him from a sea of self-doubt. A moment later, I turned back onto Western Avenue and continued toward Florence and Normandie.

A weak smile broke through the worry on her face; she lowered her head and moved it slowly from side to side; we both laughed.

From her vantage point on the corner she could see the crowds of people along both Normandie and Florence. They looked like people gathering to watch a parade. Occasionally, from the north and east, came the deep, dull thud of hard objects striking thin metal and then cracking against concrete. There was the hard-rain sound of safety glass bursting on upholstery and flesh which would soundlessly absorb its velocity. Even from a distance, these sounds were loud enough to quicken the pace of the crowd hurrying past, toward the thoroughfares.

This woman stood watching silently as though she were on the banks of a rapid, predictable river, as I and so many others flowed past her home. Though she no guarantee that this angry river would not swell, leap its banks and consume whatever lay in its path, the woman not seek refuge. Possibly she remained standing there because she felt a kinship

If I am not for myself, who will be for me?
And if I am only for myself, what am I?
And if not now, when?

HILLEL THE ELDER
THE ETHICS OF THE FATHERS

4.
THE BATTERED FACES
OF MY BROTHERS

    I parked my car just west of Bri
Street, which runs north and south,
to Normandie Avenue, and started
east, toward Normandie. A well-gro
tyish African-American woman
ing on the corner of 71st and
child of four or five twirling
her feet. She appeared to b
directions at once, swivellir
body in circles, pausing tc
eye on her child. Her vig
that she seemed as m?
the homes and lawns
told me that she lived

    As I drew clos
said, "Kind of lik
huh?"

with this river's troubled waters, and knew
the twists and turns of its long, difficult
journey. She was well-dressed and obviously
well-cared-for; but perhaps she did not
want to distance herself from this stream.
Because it is hard to turn away from a
mirror which reflects and thus chronicles
the richness, as well as the ravages, of time.

And so we smiled at each other, the
woman and I, then chuckled and shook our
heads. We didn't mention this river that
flowed through us and around us to an
angry and violent sea which might, before
day's end, destroy us both.

I spotted only a handful of the people
who lived on the street as I walked north
toward Florence. It was just a little past six,
and most were probably still stuck in rush
hour traffic or staying sensibly behind
closed doors. Three houses from the corner, I was astounded by the sight of a middle-aged man pruning flowers near the
front wall of his home while, well within his field of vision, just a few short yards
to the north, bricks and bottles crashed
loudly against moving cars and onto the
pavement.

I hailed the honey-skinned man, asking permission to enter his yard. He waved me over with a smile.

"So whaddaya think?" I asked.

He took a sip of his beer, tucked his gardening tool under his armpit, then leaned in close with a raised finger, poised for punctuation, near my chin. "Hell, I've been living with this kinda mess all my life," he said, frowning. "I come to Los Angeles in the fifties; ain't too much different now than it was then. So, see...I ain't surprised. Folks is mad. What'd they expect? I coulda told em them boys wasn't gonna do a day!"

After giving me this inside tip, he laughed out loud and took another sip of his beer. We stood together quietly for a moment, looking north into the street. I told him I thought he had a nice house. He very politely thanked me, and I thanked him for the conversation and for growing those flowers.

As I walked down the driveway, I couldn't help but think of the first line of Kipling's "If": "If you can keep your head when all about you are losing theirs..."

When I was a kid, it was standard reading in our house.

I didn't want to condemn this man for his apparent indifference to those who were literally and figuratively losing their heads less than a block from his home. I suspected that he had come of age in a time when his flower bed and his home, his small piece of the American dream, had to be hewn from the rock of racism. Perhaps, I thought, his life's labor had so exhausted his spirit that he had nothing left with which to confront the new beast that howled at the base of his driveway.

Stepping onto Florence a block west of Normandie was like stepping into another world. Above me a flock of barely noticed helicopters circled round and round the late afternoon sky. Some were TV helicopters chasing Pulitzers and ratings; others were police helicopters—I don't know what they were chasing. Earthbound black morale-boosters in passenger cars cruised the debris-littered street, feverishly beating the air with raised arms and clenched fists. At moments, an arm would lock in its outstretched position, holding the elevated fist motionless. Almost immediately, a multi-tude of bare brown arms would snap toward the late-afternoon sky in a salute of solidarity.

I had not seen this Black Power salute in many years, that feared and much-ma-ligned symbol which had lifted my young spirit during the sixties. As I stood on that corner, I realized how much I had missed that proud symbol of self-determination. This new sighting made my heart swell, and for a moment my blood ran hot with old images of defiant black Olympians herald-ing a brand-new day.

A few yards to my right an old three-quarter-ton pickup, its front wheels on the sidewalk, smoldered and burned. Thirty or forty yards to the west a subcompact sat stripped and askew in the middle of the eastbound lane. En route to the intersec-tion, I had nearly run head-on into this mechanized road kill. I had not expected it to be there in a stream of moving traffic.

On the intersection's northeast corner, thick clouds of smoke rose from a burn-ing liquor store. Flames leaped high and low from the building's roof and east wall. Even so, people continued to enter the burning store, emerging with armloads of its contents, bursting back through the entrance victorious and unscathed like modern-day Shadrachs, Meshachs, and Abednegos.

Directly in front of me, a Latino man in a small battered light-blue car shielded his face with his forearm as he swerved through sporadic barrages of bricks and bottles that landed solidly against their mark. With each multiple impact, the man bobbed and weaved at the wheel like a boxer on the ropes. With each "bob" he would inevitably lose sight of the road, and thus, temporarily, control of his vehicle. For a few seconds the car careened wildly from one lane to the other, then the top of the driver's head weaved to the surface again, eyes just above the dashboard. He had just enough time to bring the car under control before the next barrage of bricks forced a repetition of this daredevil performance.

The Florence Avenue gauntlet ran east and west of Normandie for nearly one hundred yards. The Normandie passage began at the light on the north side of the intersection, and was nearly fifty yards shorter. If a driver were skillful and frightened enough to lay on the gas and go for broke, he would probably survive the run. The truth of what might happen to those who could not successfully navigate the course was evidenced by the burning and blackened metal carcasses lying in the street. Many hours later as the entire intersection smoked and burned, I was to find further tragic evidence of unsuccessful passages: insurance cards, snapshots, personal papers, broken cylinders of lipstick and eye shadow, and a small orange overnight bag with the name Reginald Denny on the I.D. tag.

Above and behind me several faces peered over the eight-foot cinderblock wall of an automotive repair shop. The shop's gate, which faced west on Brighton, was closed and locked. From their multi-directional vantage point atop the wall, the half-dozen onlookers watched events unfold around them.

As I stood at the base of the wall, a short, thin, ruby-eyed couple sauntered toward me. They were arguing. Each carried an open brown quart bottle half concealed inside a brown paper bag. They wore shiny, greasy jeans. Their faces were drawn and grey, their hair sparse and matted. A disaffected grin exposed the fact that several of the woman's teeth were missing, and the rest were rotten and crooked. Her companion walked with a shallow dip which (if memory serves) was meant to be rhythmic, but the malt liquor had stolen his meter as well as his equilibrium, and with each step it appeared that he would stumble in mid-"dip." They appeared to take no notice of the goings-on around them. They simply strolled together down the sidewalk, alternately grinning and fussing at each other between throaty sucks at oblivion.

Lots of folks were drinking that day. In fact, the stale sweet scent of alcohol permeated the air. The signs of this old acquaintance saddened me. And I knew that before day's end it would betray dozens whose sick hospitality could do nothing but welcome it into the sanctity of their bodies with the selfish hope that, this time, the rapacious guest would leave as much as he was certain to take.

I began moving east toward the corner of Normandie, stepping cautiously past the burning pickup on the sidewalk, sure that its gas tank would explode at any moment, and amazed that so many people seemed to be oblivious to this possibility. The corner was packed, but I managed to steady myself against a light pole while the shoulder-to-shoulder crowd constantly realigned itself on the sidewalk. Most folks were just watching the goings-on, oohing and aahing in amazement each time a would-be pro-leaguer stepped off the curb preparing to throw. Most barrages began with one seemingly courageous soul hopping into the street on one leg, bottle or brick poised overhead, like a quarterback about to throw a pass. The moment the projectile hit its mark, others would rush forward to demonstrate their skill, sometimes gesturing in triumph at a particularly accurate or damaging hit.

At Florence and Normandie, there were no placards, no chants or freedom songs, and few angry faces. It occurred to me as I stood on the southwest corner of that urban high ground that this was not a protest, but a sort of coup, whose participants and supporters now luxuriated in the soft sweet bed of power. For them, this was not a time of sorrow, but a time of joy and release.

Stripped of dignity, denied equal protection and justice under the law, devalued by and on behalf of the guardians of justice, some had, as humans will, opted for the immediate gratification of retribution through terrorism. From their godlike sidewalk perch, they held the power of life and death over any and all who dared to pass their way. The centurions of peace who had beaten us and then beaten us had not shown their faces. Their birds of prey hovered powerlessly, ineffectually above us. The stamp of worthlessness that the jury's verdict had put upon us, and the image of helplessness brought home to us by a crawling, cowering young black man were both for the moment blotted out of our reality. Invalidated by violence from the slave trade to the San Gabriel Valley, and ten thousand beatings and lynchings in between, many now embraced the violent acts of others in a spontaneous attempt to affirm their humanity.

There were those too on that corner who danced with violence daily, who had long ago locked themselves behind walls of rage and self-loathing. For them the use of violence and the intimidation of the weak and frightened had become a way of life. Some of them had already begun to seize the events of April 29, 1992, as an opportunity to elevate themselves to the status of champions.

I understood clearly what was happening and why. A part of me wanted it to happen, spurred by the remaining shards of self-righteous indignation that scraped at my insides. But if I had raised my hand against another, when my rage was spent and I could no longer recall with sufficient clarity the justifications that had driven me to such brutality and horror, what would I do? How would I survive the shame and self-hatred which would overtake me as the battered faces of my brothers bled and pleaded in my memory?

In Germany they came first for the Communists, and I didn't speak up because I wasn't a Communist. Then they came for the Jews, and I didn't speak up because I wasn't a Jew. Then they came for the trade unionists, and I didn't speak up because I wasn't a trade unionist. Then they came for the Catholics, and I didn't speak up because I was a Protestant. Then they came for me, and by that time no one was left to speak up.

MARTIN NIEMOELLER

5.
MADMEN,
MUTES AND COWARDS

The windshield on the driver's side of the brown Ford Bronco segued almost invisibly from transparent ocean green to frosty white at the brick's impact. New missiles launched from three of the four street corners were already hurtling toward the two-door four-wheeler as it slammed to a stop. The driver quickly leaned right, locking the passenger door, then slammed home the lock nearest him. For a blink of an eye, it appeared that the truck's other glass barriers would hold, but a beat after the new projectiles ricocheted from them, the brittle panes shattered into a thousand hopeless pieces, and collapsed evenly from the window frame.

The corner where I stood began to boil with frightened curses. The nearly simul-

taneous impact of dozens of projectiles striking metal, glass, and pavement had caught
folks by surprise. For a few seconds, many
on the sidewalk ducked, dodged, and ran
for cover, unsure exactly where these new
sounds of danger and destruction were
coming from.

Fifty feet from the source of the violent
noise, I remained still, my back against the
light pole. A dozen or so people sprinted
toward the Bronco sitting motionless in
the middle of the intersection, ignoring
the debris that flew past their heads toward
the now nearly windowless vehicle.

"Aw shit!" someone behind me shouted
as the first blow stunned the driver in his
seat. The bottle came through the driver's
side window which had been shattered by
a metal-rod-wielding "champion" at point-
blank range. Like a starter's pistol, the
crack of the glass against the driver's skull
launched an onslaught of blows from
every direction. Someone crawled through
the windowless rear hatch and began beating the driver from behind. A tall slender
young man ran from the southwest corner, jumped through the missing passenger

window, and commenced a one-handed assault with a glass bottle, his legs dangling outside the cab.

From the first blow, the driver had been unable to protect himself. He was battered about like a sad puppet, his movements subject solely to the direction and momentum of his assailants' rage. Within fifteen or twenty seconds, the man lost consciousness, and slumped forward onto the steering wheel. Immediately, he was driven backward to an upright position by several more blows to the head.

As I watched, this brought home vividly something that had happened to me in junior high school in the spring of 1969. I was in the school auditorium; band practice was almost over, and we were waiting for the sound of the buzzer that would signal our release. I twisted apart my shiny black clarinet, swabbed out the saliva and placed the three sections snugly into the soft burgundy velveteen interior of its case. The buzzer went off. All of us began to move up the aisle of the auditorium toward our lockers to gather up our books and then board the buses for home. I was a few feet from the auditorium doors, engaging in some good-natured banter with another student, when some hard object—like a rock—slammed against my mouth: the flesh burst into bleeding pulp against my teeth. The strength of the blow, combined with the downward incline of the aisle, sent me reeling backward into the students behind me. They parted like the Red Sea. I fell over some seats, righted myself and touched two trembling fingers to the pain in my mouth. I could feel the flesh hanging from where my bottom lip had been.

Dazed and bleeding, I staggered back and forth across the aisle, trying to understand what had happened. I was frightened by the feel of my own blood, wet and sticky on my hands. I caught a blurry glimpse of someone standing laughing in the middle of the aisle. I couldn't make out his face, but he was huge. It turned out later that he was a big eighteen-year-old from a high school several miles away. Some kids were standing at the edges of the aisle, others had gathered up ahead and were watching silently from the double doors of the auditorium. A few joined my assailant in laughter. I careened wildly about the auditorium —a pitiful, helpless, hurt child. I didn't know who my assailant was, or why he had struck me. And I had lost my clarinet. I was hoping desperately that someone in this "enlightened landscape" would help me. Help me get away from that huge laughing figure, away from my shame and from those who watched me as I staggered about, bloody and afraid. Eventually a teacher came and helped me to the office.

A few days later, as I sat, stitched and swollen, in the vice principal's office, I came to understand what had happened, for the vice principal said that I had come to his school "walking too tall" and holding my head "a little too high and many of the students resented it. So," he said to my mother, "of course, what could you expect?"

Only a short time before I had transferred to this school from a predominantly black school in Des Moines, where I had not seemed to fit in: my "ethnicity" had been questioned, so to speak. I wasn't an athlete, I liked to play the piano, and I "talked funny." I thought I would be happier here. Now I was overwhelmed with despair at the discovery that in this Middle-American educational institution—where I was one of two African-American students— I was not respected as a human being. It was not my ethnicity that was questioned, but my humanity. I carried the scar of the incident for twenty-five years—not only physically, but psychologically, because through it I lost a trusted friend. I realized only recently that I haven't played the clarinet since that day in the auditorium.

Now the vivid memory of that beating and abandonment, some twenty-five years ago, propelled me into the intersection. I remembered too well the feelings I had had, the hurtful words and images—I could not accept this attack, the suffering of this human being. It seemed that he and I had become one, that his suffering and mine, present and past, had fused, and with one loud and silent voice now cried for help within this single irretrievable moment.

My conscience heard our cry, and carried me forward to preserve justice for him and to reclaim justice for myself.

I moved neither slowly nor quickly, not in anger but in extreme sorrow. Sorrow for those who were seeing, but who could not see; sorrow for the ones who saw but who had lost the ability to feel; sorrow for the hated and for those who nurtured hate with their silence. Although the man in the intersection was being robbed of his existence, my sorrow was not for death, but for the prevailing misery of life, and grew from a remembrance of the ache that comes with knowing that one has been exiled from the human heart.

"Come on, ya'll . . . ya'll know this ain't right," I said to several people jockeying for striking positions at the driver's side of the truck. One fellow had his hand on the latch, and was about to open the door. I looked squarely into the eyes of another who had just landed a blow to the driver's face. The bottle he was holding chest high dropped immediately to his side. He took a small step backward, bumping into a short, stout, middle-aged black man, who, with his back and right leg pinned against the vehicle, and his arms outstretched, was trying to hold people back and away from the truck while he pleaded for the driver's life. "Please, please! Don't do this. Please don't hurt him no more!"

The would-be assailant behind me had begun to open the door. With my left hand I gripped the door frame, pushed the door fully open, stepped in between the driver and his attackers, reached inside the cab, and grabbed the unconscious victim under the arms. "Come on man, let's go," I said. I could barely make out, through the blood, that he was of Asian descent. He was heavy and it took a moment to get a solid grip on him. I pulled hard and held my body against his back in order to ease his drop from the truck cab to the street, my face pressed against his blood-soaked hair. Suddenly the light which was coming through the window frame on the passenger side was blotted out by a large figure leaping head first into the cab. Simultaneously, a glass bottle shattered against the Asian man's face, spraying stinging shards across my left cheek.

For a few brief moments, time seemed to slow down tremendously; I felt as if my body and everything around me was moving at half speed. I had been calm as I walked toward the truck. But now, as I felt the tiny particles of glass clinging to my skin, real time resumed, and adrenaline drove me backward and away from the vehicle with my unconscious and bloody stranger firmly in tow. I was praying that my legs would carry us far enough, fast enough, to escape the next blow.

After seeing the man being so easily jostled around the cab of the truck, I was surprised that his unconscious form was so heavy. Because he was so heavy, we were not moving fast enough to outrun the mob. Six or seven feet from the Bronco, a young man ran toward us, bottle in hand, cocking his arm for a hit. I knew what was coming. With all my strength I tried to turn the driver's limp body away from the direction of the attack. Sadly, I was too slow. The beer bottle disintegrated almost silently against the man's already unrecognizable face.

Anger and revulsion leaped into my throat as I watched his assailant scurry away toward the anonymity of the crowd. I cringed at the youngster's cowardice. My

arms had been full, my charge unconscious—what had this "brave" young "champion" to fear? Why had he not stood his
righteous ground? Why had he struck a
man unable to defend himself, and then
run away? Surely this was not the way of
a "noble warrior, avenger of injustice, pro-
tector of the race."

For an instant I wanted to hurt him, as
he had hurt someone else. I wanted to
shake him until he woke from the senseless
and bitter nightmare that had terrorized
his spirit, and so wickedly altered his reality. I wanted to make him understand that
he was the seed of a courageous and com-
passionate people. And, that although his
American ancestors were often hard pressed
for life's essentials, and sometimes for life
itself, he was infinitely poorer than they.
Because unlike those before him, he was
now a man without honor. I wished that I
could force open his eyes, so that he could
look clearly at his victim, and see the truth
about himself.

My anger subsided, replaced by a sad
awareness that the sick and brutal young
man might never perceive the spiritual

self-destructiveness of his inhumanity. Perhaps in bitter years to come, as he sought to blame others for his discontent, he would somehow come to comprehend that it is most often our own actions which power the wheels of our fate. If he were very lucky, one day he might be shown, as I had been, that the millstone of dishonor often far exceeds the weight of injustice. For dishonor, self-imposed, grates heavily upon the conscience, and crushes the spirit.

I pulled the still-unconscious man to the sidewalk, laid him on the pavement, and held his head in my hands. He appeared to be coming to, so with urgency, I asked, "Can you walk?"

He shook his head. No.

"Well, you gotta walk or you're gonna die," I told him, lifting him back to his feet.

He was more than wobbly, but managed to hold himself up long enough for me to get one arm around his waist, and his right arm over my shoulder. Unable to see for the blood which ran freely into his eyes, semi-conscious and beaten nearly beyond recognition, miraculously he began to put one foot in front of the other as I

guided him down the sidewalk. He held
on to me the way a drowning man clings to
a life preserver. And then he looked at me
in a way that seemed so familiar—I had
seen it somewhere before, but couldn't
place it. The look came from deep within
him, a look that said "thanks," and "congratulations," all at once. Suddenly, I experienced a buoyant and peaceful feeling, a
mood so confident and gentle that I knew
our communion was a celebration of life.
And that, if we survived, from this day forward, we would have that life more abun-
dantly.

"What's your name?" I asked him.

I attributed his unintelligible answer to
the thickness of a foreign accent and assumed that he was a recent immigrant.

"Welcome to America," I said with a
smile. Later I realized that he could not
speak because his lips were torn and broken.
I also found out later that this American
had been born in a government internment
camp during the Second World War, and
that he had grown up not far from this very
street. In response to my mistaken welcome, he raised the one eye which had not

swelled shut, and through shattered blood-caked lips, and broken teeth, flashed me a small painful grin.

"Yeah, you Korean motherfucker, got what you deserved, that's for Latasha Harlins!" a teenage girl screamed as she passed to our right on the sidewalk, referring to the Los Angeles teenager who had been killed by a Korean grocer the previous year. The angry girl's companion stood wide-eyed as we approached, then covered her own gaping, speechless mouth with one hand, closed her eyes, and rushed past us, unable to look upon the face of vengeance.

As we moved down the sidewalk, people parted to let us by. Their expressions varied from shock and horror to broad smiles and indifferent stares. Some burst into tears at the sight of the wounded man. Others, calloused by a brutal existence, glanced in our direction, and continued their curbside conversations.

The houses along this block of Florence have no front yards, and sit only a side-walk's width from the street. One elderly African-American woman stepped onto her front porch as we struggled by, caught an extreme close-up of my companion and screamed. She was close enough to touch, and I saw her eyes swell with tears as she offered to call 911. "Please," I said, but kept moving. Bricks and other debris flew toward us constantly, and my only thought was to get us both as far from the area as possible.

I had left the gym wearing my work-out clothes: red gym shorts, tank top, a biker's cap with a turned-up visor, and a pair of dark sunglasses. I was glad that it had been chest-and-back day in the weight room. Since my upper body was pumped, I was hoping that I didn't look like an easy mark to the "hunters" who appeared to be choosing their prey, in part, based on its apparent inability to defend itself. As we walked, I concentrated on maintaining my "street" face: a look devoid of emotion, hoping that the dark glasses would conceal the fear in my eyes. My head turned neither left nor right; I kept my eyes straight ahead. Now and then, I looked over my shoulder for danger coming from behind.

My friend was getting heavier. I needed to find a safe place for a moment's rest.

On our right, in the middle of the block, we turned into a driveway that led to a small apartment building which stood in back of the commercial property that fronted the street. To my left, I noticed another building with rear steps which were not visible from Florence. Relieved, I ducked around the corner of the structure and made a move to set my charge down on the concrete stairs. "Hell no!" a voice from behind me hollered. "Get him the hell out of here!" Across the driveway, a small tan-skinned man struck firmly at the air with the back of his hand, gesturing for us to go away.

"Huh uh . . . you can't bring him up in here," he said shaking his head vigorously. "Get him the hell away from here!"

I figured we had enough trouble, so I didn't argue. I picked my friend up again and headed back out to the street. The man's female companion began to plead with him on our behalf, but he refused to listen. I sensed, however, that her words had affected him, for as we resumed our journey, we passed directly in front of him and even as he continued to order us off his property, he could no longer look at us. He literally turned his back as he drove us away with his fear.

"Accomplish the mission!"

"Sir, accomplish the mission, aye aye sir!" Our shouted response to the drill instructor's command reverberated in my memory as my friend went in and out of consciousness. My body ached with his weight, but there could be no stopping, not on this street. Accomplish the mission.

During the first few hours of boot camp I would have reneged on my deal with Uncle Sam, if there had been an easy way out. Each morning during the mandatory three-mile run, I routinely dropped out well before the midway point. My drill instructors, Staff Sergeant Turner and Sergeant Doran, alternately harassed, tugged, and generally "encouraged" me not to give up. "One day," they said, "the lives of your fellow Marines, the very men you're training with, could depend on your staying the course, no matter how tired you get." And no matter how many times I gave up during that run, those drill instructors never left me behind, never stopped pushing and pulling me toward my responsibility. Ultimately, one morning I moved across that three-mile line in stride with my peers, and in spite of myself.

Again, I had been shown that I could do what I had believed I could not do.

That afternoon, a block and a half east of an intersection where a young truck driver had nearly been murdered in broad daylight, the courageous dedicated spirit of two heroes named Turner and Doran joined together with the energies of other heroines and heroes who had been gathering that day on my behalf. Among them were a young mother from rural Mississippi, a house painter, an ex-highroller, a Catholic layworker, an impoverished Indian woman and her handicapped child, a retired postal worker, saints, ministers, priests, and friends whose surnames I don't know. In the midst of the longest run of my life, when I was tired, scared, and, except for the battered man at my side, very much alone, their voices strengthened and beckoned me toward the finish line.

By the grace of God, and their wisdom and courage, my new friend and I continued to move steadily through the fire.

"Set him down man, set him down, he's bleedin bad," urged the man at the corner two blocks from Normandie, as he ushered us into a side street. I sat my friend on the grass and a middle-aged woman timidly offered a paper towel to wipe his wounds, then quickly returned to safety in the house behind us. Two or three gaunt men conferenced a short distance away, lamenting his injuries and shaking their heads in disbelief. Against the advice of a friend standing nearby, one fellow suggested I bring my charge into his home, a few doors down. I respectfully declined. I didn't know the man and if my friend and I were attacked, I reasoned that it would be better if it happened in full view of the public.

I attempted to apply pressure to my friend's wounds, but he kept turning his head deliriously in every direction trying to get some sense of where he was.

"Don't turn around man, look at me," I said firmly. I wanted as few people as possible to realize that he was not African-American.

A small crowd stood on the corner a

few yards to our left, looking up towards the Florence and Normandie intersection. Cars continued to cruise slowly up and down Florence, blasting their horns in solidarity with those on the sidewalks. Many of the passengers leaned out of the windows, smiling broadly. Now and again, a projectile would come hurtling across the street, over the heads of those on the corner, and land just inches from where my friend and I were sitting on the grass.

After several minutes, a great shout went up from the corner: a black-and-white police cruiser had passed, headed toward the intersection, and the bystanders were hailing the officers on our behalf. The squad car backed up, turned, and pulled to a stop in front of us. I smiled when I spoke to them, glad that my mission was nearly accomplished. "This guy's hurt bad, he needs help," I said.

The black officer behind the wheel and his white female partner were silent. They stared at us for twenty or thirty seconds; then, without gesture or word, they drove away. Immediately, adrenaline started losing ground to the fear not so deep inside me. I couldn't believe it. I had kept walking in the certainty that eventually, in the midst of this madness, I would run into a cop or a paramedic. And I had been right, but now they were driving away, and I was so stunned I couldn't even cry out after them. I watched as they made a U-turn at the next intersection and headed back toward us. Again they stopped and looked. The black cop was talking on the radio. The female cop, blond with a Gibson Girl hairstyle, looked at us over the ridge of the seat. The male cop was wearing his "street face," but I could tell that the woman officer was concerned. The look on her face said she wanted to help us, but was somehow prevented from doing so. That look stayed on her face, even as her partner pulled off for the second and final time.

My world went spinning. I thought about my children, and the things I had yet to do. I cursed the officers and reviled them as they turned the corner and sped east. "Oh yes," I sneered, "if it's one lone nigger groveling on the ground, no problem! If it's twenty to one with sticks, tasers and nine-millimeters you guys are 'good to go.' But if the odds ain't in your favor, baby—time to go!"

Although the officers had abandoned us, and their sworn oath to serve and protect, I might not have been so disillusioned if both the officers were white. But even though I had no right to do so, I had expected better from the black man in blue. At that moment, I speculated angrily that his initiation into the "fraternal order" long ago demanded that he abandon the people on this corner—an embarrassment to such a one as he, officer of the law, and "credit to his race." As for my friend of Japanese descent, his condition was such that it was difficult to tell what race he was. Perhaps to the officers, we were just two sorry, expendable "niggers" in the hood, too far gone to be worth risking personal safety or career by violating orders.

With the departure of the officers, it became clear to all that chaos reigned. The kind fellow who had previously implored me to set the injured man on his grass now strongly suggested that I take him elsewhere. Those who had lamented his condition moments before now moved as far

away from us as they could get. The concerned fellow who had offered refuge in
his home now demanded in no uncertain
terms that we remove ourselves from the
proximity of his abode. Those who had
summoned the officers quickly dispersed,
shaking their heads in regret, and leaving
my friend and me in clear view of the hostile traffic on Florence.

In a reality ruled by madmen, mutes,
and cowards, I pulled my friend to his feet
and contemplated a new journey. Again he
began to turn deliriously, this way and that.
"Don't move, damn it, just don't move," I
demanded. I held him close like a lover,
locking him in an embrace to keep him
motionless. We could not turn back. To go
north we would have to cross Florence. Con-
tinuing east would take us further from the
violence but toward what, I could not be
sure. The residential road to the south was
empty. As far as I could see there were only
locked and quiet homes. No crowds, no
traffic, just an occasional weary-looking
"revolutionary," sidestepping and glancing
over his shoulder as he spirited a case of
looted liquor toward some hiding place. So

south we went, arm over a shoulder, arm around a waist. We had traveled only a short distance when I noticed the blood flowing dark and steady from my friend's left ear.

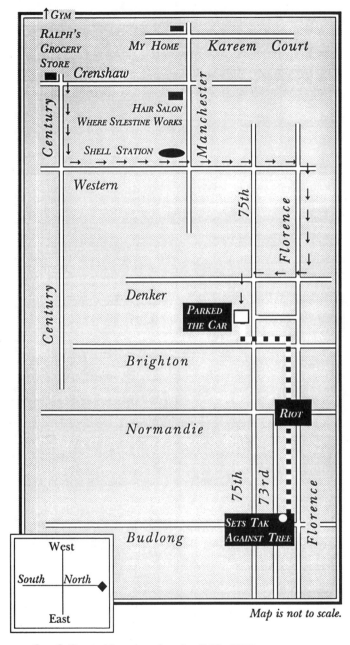

Map is not to scale.

South Central Los Angeles: April 29, 1992

Gregory dragging Takao Hirata from his truck as an attacker strikes with a bottle

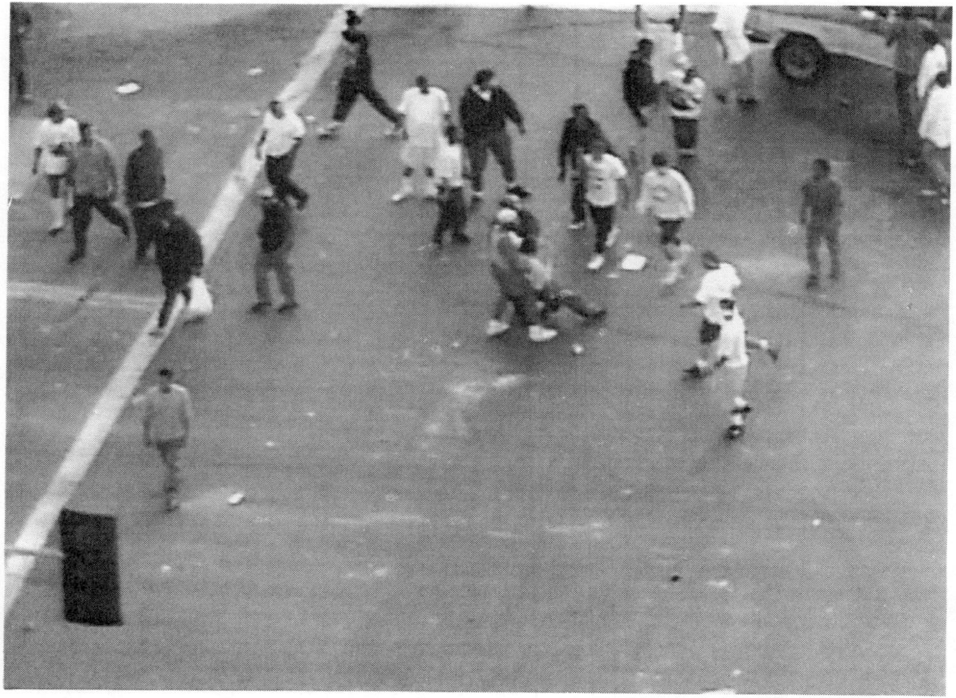

(Courtesy KNBC)

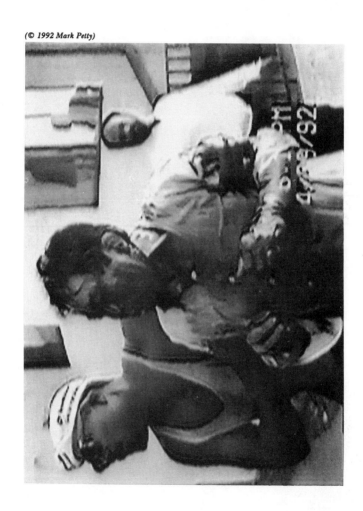

Motorist attacked with a Molotov cocktail

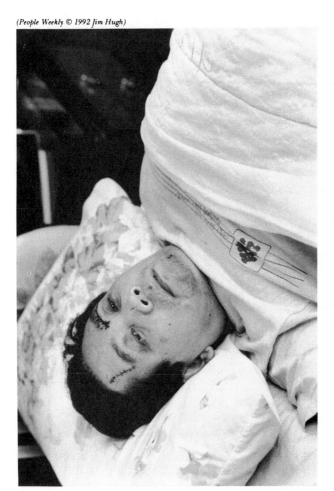

Takao Hirata at the Metropolitan Medical Center

(Bob Galbraith/ AP/ Wide World Photo)

After giving an emotional speech to the Los Angeles City Council

Testifying in the trial of Damion Williams and Henry Watson

Semper Fidelis

U. S. Marine Corps Motto

6.
UNAUTHORIZED ACTIVITY

Once on a warm fall night, three months after my eighteenth birthday, I was shaken from a deep exhausted sleep by various hands. When I had raised myself up on my elbows and forearms, the hunched-over young recruits moved on to the next of the small steel beds which we called "racks."

Through the large rectangular windows that comprised much of the squad bay's north and south walls, the soft blue light of the autumn moon illuminated the sixty or so skivvy-clad aspiring Marines who were still asleep. But across the squad bay, recruits were rising up like B-movie zombies, lifting stiff unrested legs slowly up and away from the rack, then easing swollen and blistered feet onto the cold dark tile floor. Several of my waking comrades wore Cheshire grins, others winked sleepily at ones close by. Just moments after opening my eyes, I saw the "firewatch" slip out the door. It was his job to sound the alarm in the event of fire, or any other "unusual" or "UA"—unauthorized—activity. The firewatch knew, as we all did, that this temporary departure from his post was punishable by court martial.

I delayed as long as I thought possible without arousing suspicion, then pulled my knees underneath me, rocked backward to an upright position and stepped sideways out of bed.

The suspicions I was being careful to suppress were my own, for there had been moments when I feared that I might not really belong among this fraternity of men— the few, the proud. There were terrifying moments when, in my mind, I had come dangerously close to acknowledging my discomfort with terms like "gook" and "nip," and my distrust of superiors who casually mixed these slurs with words like "freedom" and "honor."

I moved into the aisle behind three recruits who carried thick green wool blankets rumpled tightly in their arms. Several other barefoot, nearly bald, faceless figures in baggy stark-white boxer shorts and t-shirts approached silently from all directions toward a row of racks near the south windows. By the light of the moon, even the sons of Africa among us looked like pale sinister ghouls.

A few feet ahead of me, several recruits had already surrounded the rack of the platoon's most feared and despised "nonhacker."

Private Ladieu's mouth gaped wide, the rattling intake of each unearned, self-satisfied snore drawing us closer to the task at hand. An entire range of seeping, pink inflammations at the point of bursting rose from the private's pores. The sight of this scarred and cratered landscape outraged our now sleep-deprived sense of decency as never before.

Ladieu's unwillingness to give himself completely and totally to the good of the platoon had angered and confused us. Why wouldn't he cooperate, we wondered? Why the hell wouldn't he polish his filthy brass, shine his scuzzy shoes, and humbly give his last ounce of voice and strength to the will of the divine eagle, globe and anchor? If only he would become one of us, I thought, as the blankets were tossed over his still slumbering form.

"Semper Fi, you son of a bitch," someone else whispered, as I and the others began to beat him with our fists.

Ladieu's unsuspecting wool-encased body stiffened in shock beneath the impact of the first blows. Instinctively he tried to raise himself, and several of us pushed him down again. The rapid, uncoordinated, unceasing blows continued. Biting my lower lip, I lifted myself up on tiptoes, raised my right arm high above my head and aimed carefully, like a kamikaze.

As Ladieu writhed and screamed on the bed, contradictions battled inside me. The self-righteousness of my blows kept my guilt at bay, but, between blows, I was overcome by a rush of decency, which threatened to expose me in front of my peers, and damage the warrior image I had fashioned for myself.

As the soft flesh cringed under the flailing fists, my heart splintered into smaller and smaller dehumanizing fragments. Like a celluloid wolfman, I was both terrified and disgusted by the monster I had become, but my senses were overwhelmed by the scent of frightened and defenseless blood which promised, and indeed delivered, an invigorating fix of supremacy and power. Like a real life Lon Chaney character, I had been unwittingly cursed and now, self-image, esteem, and consequently behavior were being shaped and driven by forces outside my good conscience.

From the beginning Ladieu's suffering had seeped through each brutal knuckle of my fist. Not only could I see, but I could feel the torment inflicted by my fear and lust for power—yet being the selfish coward that I was, I did not seek, and therefore could not find, the courage to stop.

Sometime during the second minute of the beating someone returned with a web belt and buckle and began swinging viciously toward the place where Private Ladieu's head seemed to be. With each strike of the belt's buckle, Ladieu shrieked like a small child, then thrashed and begged beneath the blankets in terrified anticipation of the next blow. Those screams and the whoosh of the belt as it bullied the air from its path slowed our battering to an occasional half-hearted punch, accompanied by a soft grunt of spent resentment. Then, for most of us, it was simply over.

No words were spoken as we departed to our racks, no words had passed our lips the entire time. Those who had brought blankets snatched them away quickly and hurried back to their sleeping places.

It is impossible to say exactly where the idea of the blanket party originated, but somehow it became planted in our minds just a few days before the attack on our hapless comrade.

Private Ladieu had been singled out as a "non-hacker" and so-called "scuzball" during the early weeks of recruit training. Like me, Ladieu always fell out of the morning run, but in spite of the drill instructors' efforts he showed no improvement and appeared to lack even the will to try. On the rifle range the uncoordinated private rarely hit even the edges of the target. Once, on the pistol range, Ladieu lost control of a .45 caliber automatic, sending live rounds dangerously close to his fellow recruits until he was tackled by the Range Master. Ladieu's brass was always brown, his uniform wrinkled and unkempt. The drill instructors considered his skin problem a sign of uncleanliness, and in fact Ladieu's showers lasted only a moment.

Because of our fellow recruit's intransigence we had all suffered. When Ladieu did not clean himself thoroughly, or stay in step during drill, the entire platoon of eighty men was made to do endless push-ups until we were unable to lift our arms. If Private Ladieu did not properly wash and starch his uniform, we would soon find ourselves face down in the mud, chewing mouthfuls of dirt and chanting, "Thank you, Private Ladieu," over and over again.

That night the word had gone around the squad bay from squad leader to squad leader just before lights out: "Blanket party for Ladieu tonight."

The idea of several people beating up on one person didn't suit me very well. I had fled that threat myself a few times. I didn't really take the plan seriously. We

were, after all, training to be United States
Marines, and there were issues of duty,
honor, and faithfulness to consider. Certainly twenty against one would not be an
honorable thing. But the blanket party had
been held.

I climbed back into bed, stretched out
on my back, stared at the ceiling, and tried
to empty my mind of what I had just done.
I calmly attempted to summon and hold
the rationale that Ladieu had gotten what
he deserved, but the delusion kept slipping
away, until finally it would not come at
all. Then, slightly desperate, I reasoned
that he had not really been hurt at all! A
bit frightened perhaps, and it might have
even done him some good! These ludicrous
rationalizations brought the savagery of
the scene bursting in upon me, forcing me
to seek refuge beneath my blanket. There
in the hot small darkness I continued to
hear and feel Ladieu's torment. I placed a
pillow over my head to block out his moans.
I squeezed my eyes closed, and clenched
my fists as tightly as I could, in a futile
attempt to push his anguish from my
present and my past. Despite these efforts

to preserve my innocence, truth pene-
trated my being like hard and unrelenting
rain through a window screen. Shame and
remorse seeped unconstrained through
every pore and then sorrow made me shiver
with tears. For the love of Jesus, what had
I done? Over and over beneath the covers
now wrapped tightly around me like a
mystical shield protecting me from the bo-
gey man of my own evil, I prayed to the
God of my childhood for redemption,
rocked like a baby, and ashamedly petition-
ed my victim for absolution, mouthing
wet, silent pleas for forgiveness, "I'm sorry,
Ladieu, please forgive me," I begged. "I'm
so sorry."

I had not been a model recruit either.
But by the time our battalion returned from
basic infantry training at Camp Pendleton,
my physical abilities had grown miraculously; not only could I run, but I often led
the songs and cadence calls which mo-
tivated us up and down the steep dirt roads
of Camp Pendleton: "Your corps...Our
corps . . . Hard corps . . . Marine corps."

My zeal earned me the title of Platoon
Guide, and the honor of bearing its colors.

The position of Guide was a most coveted prize, a prize I had never imagined I either could, or would, possess. Each day as I strutted across the parade deck, a step ahead of my platoon, it was all I could do to suppress a "UA" grin that originated somewhere in my stomach and grew to gargantuan proportions as it rose through my chest and neck and threatened to burst uncontrollably over my entire face. I have arrived, I thought. I was one of the fellas, a warrior, a man, and I knew as I marched that I would unquestioningly do anything to preserve this blessed state of being.

And so to keep my place among these men, a place which I had so often dreamed of and desperately craved, I took my place among the mob. Not because I was overcome with hatred, or anger, but because I was flushed with a fear which flowed like oxygen through every vessel and cell, an invisible but potent substance which brought moral anesthesia to heart and mind.

The following morning, a Sunday, Private Ladieu did not fall out for morning chow. He merely sat motionless on his green, trunk-shaped ditty box.

After returning from the mess hall, we took our places on our own ditty boxes and began the Sunday ritual of spit and polish, letter-writing and laundry. In the midst of these brief hours of personal freedom, Private Ladieu initiated a ritual of his own. He stood up, raised a can of brass polish to his lips and drank. After a few gulps he sat down, calmly. It was as if he had re-seated himself upon a playground teeter-totter as recruits up and down the line popped to attention and began yelling in quick, orderly succession, "Sir! Private Ladieu just drank a can of Brasso, Sir!"

"Sir! Private Ladieu just drank a can of Brasso, Sir!"

"Sir! Private Ladieu just drank a can of Brasso, Sir!"

During these hysterical but disciplined cries for help, Ladieu gagged, dropped the can, and clutched his belly. As the drill instructors emerged from the duty hut, the private lurched forward and screamed. "Goddammit, Ladieu!" Drill Instructor Staff Sergeant Turner yelled as Ladieu sprinted toward the open stairwell.

By the time our superiors began their pursuit, Ladieu had already climbed atop the highest railing and, before any of us could say his name and rank again, he was airborne, beginning his descent toward the concrete deck, two stories below.

A week before graduation day, Staff Sergeant Turner said to me, "Fall out on the parade deck at thirteen-hundred, Private Williams. I want you in the battalion color guard for graduation."

I beamed. "Sir, yes, Sir!"

"You just might be the first black private to carry the American flag for this battalion, Williams. The first since I've been on the drill field. Whaddaya think about that, Private?"

"It's quite an honor, Sir!"

"Yes indeedy, Private. Yes indeedy. Dissmissed!"

Actually I was not the first black Marine to carry the colors in this boot camp or any other. Up until the early fifties, black Marines had their own Marine Corps Recruit Training Depot—Montford Point, North Carolina. By 1974 most of the black

Marines I met who had over twenty years service were Montford Point Marines, as they called themselves. But much of their courageous history, like the courageous history of Africans in America, has been forgotten or ignored.

Although I knew the Marine Corps had been segregated, I believed that being singled out to bear the nation's colors was something to be proud of. The moment I joined the Marine Corps I had forgiven America, if I had not forgotten its misdeeds. Like so many other African-American men and women before me I was sure that my willingness to serve, to kill, to die in defense of freedom or simply on command, would, once and for all, prove my worth and entitle me to undeniable equality beneath the democracy's blanket of broad stripes and bright stars.

That afternoon on the drill field I, along with three privates from second battalion, received instruction on color guard duty. Throughout the afternoon we were reminded of our good luck at being chosen for this honor, and of its importance. As we were marching, wheeling and pivoting

across the parade deck, we passed an uncoordinated platoon of fresh recruits. Each
was dressed in identical new green wrinkled
utility trousers, oversized grey-white sweat-
shirts which were either too large or too
small, and white sneakers. Their heads were
shaved to the scalp under their un-starched
caps and their footsteps were so out of sync
that they resembled a herd of malnourished
cattle moving across a dry, inhospitable
plain. Most kept their eyes on the asphalt,
but glanced fearfully now and then, at the
starched and irritable herdsman who belit-
tled and occasionally batted at them as they
plodded toward their barracks.

At the rear of the group an erect recruit was marching; there were remnants
of starch in his frequently washed trousers, which matched the faded green of
his shirt. His cap too was starched, unlike
the soft new caps of the others. His hair
was short, but it was still hair, and he carried
a full sea bag over his shoulder without
bending at the waist. He marched in cadence.

The Latino private marching next to
me asked, "Ain't that that one guy?"

I whispered out of the side of my mouth, "Who?"

"The one that drank the Brasso."

The scuttlebutt in the platoon was that after spending some time in sick bay, Private Ladieu had almost gotten a medical discharge for insanity. But then the Battalion Commander had decided the private wasn't really crazy after all but had just been trying to get out of the Corps. This meant, of course, according to Marine Corps standards, that Ladieu was really a coward and a non-hacker as everyone had always thought he was. Consequently, it was decided that the Corps would do the private a favor and make another attempt to turn him around. Staff Sergeant Turner told us that Ladieu was to be recycled and begin his thirteen weeks of boot camp all over again from the beginning.

So it was Private Ladieu I saw that day on the parade deck as I was learning how to carry my country's flag. He never looked at us: he just marched, head up, in step, with a bunch of kids who were out of step and ignorant of most of what lay ahead and of everything that had happened. There

was something in Ladieu's stride that day—
a resolve. This time, I think, he was deter-
mined to survive. Both because of our brutality and in spite of it. He looked willing,
as I had been, to do anything to become
a respected knight of the realm. One of the
few . . . the proud.

It aint whatcha take, it's whatcha leave.

ANONYMOUS

7.
MISSION ACCOMPLISHED

The moment I saw the blood flowing from my friend's ear, I had set him down again, with his back against a wooden light pole, only half a block from where the police had abandoned us. I wasn't sure what sort of injury the blood indicated, but at that moment I began to fear that his injuries were threatening his life.

I hoped that the light pole would hide my friend from anyone looking south from Florence long enough for me to figure out what to do. Within seconds a small blue car, full of little brown children, pulled to a stop behind me. A plump brown woman at the wheel leaned past the two children in the front seat and asked, "Do you want me to take him to the hospital?" There was little room left in the car, no way to conceal him except underneath the children. "No, that's okay," I said, "the kids might get hurt."

The woman was still for a moment, then nodded and drove off. As she pulled away, a brown Chevy van rounded the corner from Florence. "Yo man, you want me to take him to the hospital?" asked its lone occupant, a thirtyish black man wearing a black "doo rag" on his head; it hung down to his shoulders.

"Naw . . . that's all right," I said with a frown.

"You sure, partner? He looks like he's hurt pretty bad." The van driver pressed me.

I glanced at the blood still flowing from my semi-conscious friend's ear, then turned back to the driver, "You sure, man? You're gonna take him to the hospital, right?"

The man in the van seemed to appreciate my uncertainty; he became thoughtful for a moment, then replied, "For real, Black. For real."

I lifted my friend to his feet and carried him to the passenger side of the van. The driver leaned over, opened the door, and together we got him securely into the front seat.

"Thanks," I said to the driver, reaching over to shake his hand.

I had chosen to trust this "brother" because throughout our brief but urgent conversation, he had looked me directly in the eye; I had recalled Mr Bus squatting in our living room after work on a low red ottoman, talking in soft man-to-boy tones about the trustworthiness of men who looked you in the eye when they spoke, and gave a solid grip when they shook your hand.

As I shook the driver's hand, his grasp was firm, and he looked straight into my eyes again. The van pulled away, and I headed back toward the intersection along a side street.

As I walked the side street alone, back toward the intersection of Florence and Normandie, I thought again of Private Ladieu. I've thought of him often during the eighteen years since my brutality stripped him of his humanity, and drove him toward an unsuccessful attempt on his life. Now while I was single-handedly trying and convicting those who had perpetrated that day's acts of violence, the memory of my own

moral cowardice slipped into my consciousness like a hostile witness through a courtroom door. Conscience gasped, ego pro-
tested, but honesty overruled and admitted
the discomfiting truth.

My cowardice had caused me to com-
mit a shameful and barbaric act and, for
many years, the millstone of dishonor had
hung unceasing and heavy upon my spirit.
And now, simply because I had fulfilled
this particular day's responsibility to another human being, I was eager to condemn
others. As I walked, I painfully remembered
that I too had had my day as part and parcel
of the mob.

Driven by fear, insecurity, and a selfish
desperation to preserve our place among
those like ourselves, we had betrayed our
humanity—all of us. Those who beat Rodney
King, those who battered the people at
Florence and Normandie, and those like
me who participated in the beating of Private Ladieu—we had all abandoned principle and decency in the self-serving name
of order and justice.

"You okay, man?" one among a small

group of teenagers inquired as I passed.

I nodded without looking their way. Covered as I was with my friend's blood from head to toe, many passersby thought I had been injured in the violence. I thought it best not to, but I desperately wanted to tell them that the blood which looked so much a part of me had come from an Asian American whose name I didn't even know, and who was at that very moment being taken to a hospital by a lean, brown-skinned man in his mid-thirties whose name I didn't know either.

When I reached Normandie, I stood among the crowd and watched as another small car carrying three Latino passengers zigzagged through the north-south gauntlet, a path which, by then, had grown longer and more dense with onlookers. Only a few projectiles were hurled at the vehicle, and I saw at least one of the passengers grin as the car successfully reached the end of the narrowed passage and safety.

I looked north toward the intersection to see if there were any who needed help. The crossroads were clear except for the carcasses of smashed and looted vehicles.

After a few minutes I crossed the street and headed back to my car. By then several of the residents along this quiet side street were standing in their yards and doorways. A man and his teenage son stood staring at me as I opened the trunk of my car and took out a towel to wipe my face. They said nothing, and neither did I. I imagined that they were wondering who this particular interloper was; where had he come from; why was he trespassing upon their peace and privacy and helping to give their neighborhood a bad name?

Days later, more than one of the neighborhood residents would call me an outsider and a sellout. My first reaction to their words was hurt, pure and animal. And of course, then came animal anger, too. But somewhere between anger and desire for retaliation, I felt empathy—I could almost understand how these people must feel after having watched their community being looted and burned and then, in the aftermath, being unable either to claim responsibility or place it firmly where it belonged. I could more than sense what it was like to be torn between the healing and hopefulness of honest self-appraisal, and the obsolete strategies of a people born and nurtured under siege: not really believing that the enemy outside the wall is always the enemy, but simply conditioned to defend and accept the old credo that truth spoken too loudly is treason.

I stood at the open trunk of my car for a good while, asking myself whether I should return to the corner, or leave. I decided to go. My wife worked not far from the area and I thought that I should go and see about her.

I drove back down Western Avenue the way I had come. As I prepared to turn west on Manchester, thirty or forty people dashed from the sidewalk and raced across the street. Several yards ahead, a white stretch limousine sat with its entire front end inside a Foot Locker shoe store. Dozens of people were climbing over and around the white Lincoln to claim the outlet's contents. Within moments the crowd darting in front of me had joined the others in their pursuit of athletic footwear.

My wife Sylestine rented space in a small hairdressing salon on Manchester a few short blocks from the shoe store. When I was only a couple of yards from the salon's driveway, I looked in my rear-view mirror and saw smoke and flames coming from several locations a half mile or so behind me.

When I walked into the salon the half-dozen operators and clients, including my wife, stopped in mid-conversation and stared at me. The client sitting in Sylestine's chair was clearly in the early stages of whatever hair treatment she was getting, but I offered my apologies and told her politely that it was time for Sylest to go home, and that perhaps she and the others should do likewise.

Sylestine said nothing as we left the salon, even though I was bloody and disheveled. We drove our separate cars home. In the living room, I sat on the edge of the coffee table and turned on the news.

"Where've you been?" she asked quietly.

"Oh, out and about," I replied with a grin.

"I saw you on TV," she said, frowning.

"Really? When?"

"At the shop. There was a man getting

beat up, and a guy came and pulled him out of his car. One of the ladies said, 'Look! That guy's trying to help him; they're gonna kill him too!' I agreed with her. Then I took a closer look at the TV and I told my customer, 'My husband has a hat just like that.'"

We were both silent for a long time. Then Sylestine went into the bedroom and closed the door. In a few minutes I saw the footage she had seen at the shop—an aerial shot, taken from a helicopter. There I was, and my friend too, and the others.

As I watched the television news reports of the violence and looting which was breaking out all over the city, my thoughts turned to the man in the van who had taken my friend to the hospital. I was hoping that the sincerity that I read in his eyes had been genuine. I dreaded to think of what might have happened if Mr Bus were mistaken about the eyes being the window to a man's soul. If I was right about the Good Samaritan, my friend should be in a hospital by now. I grabbed the yellow pages and began calling hospitals in the area, emergency rooms. I should have gone with him, I thought, to make sure.

Fifteen or twenty minutes later Sylestine emerged from the bedroom and sat down next to me on the coffee table.

"Are you hurt anywhere?" she asked.

"No. I'm okay." I dialed another hospital. "Just a little cut on my finger."

"Let's see it." She took my hand in her lap. "Is that his blood on you?"

"Yeah."

"Don't you think you oughta get checked?"

"Checked? For what?"

"Hepatitis . . . HIV."

"Come on," I said, more than a little ticked. "Be for real."

"I am being for real. You don't know who that man is or what he does."

Syleste and I argued back and forth for a while. I told her that her concerns were cynical and ridiculous. She was getting on my nerves. "Do you think God would let me get away with what I got away with out there and then let me get AIDS!" I yelled.

"You need to get checked, Greg," my wife, the ex-navy corpsman, repeated calmly.

"Damn it, Syleste, it don't even show up for six months!"

"Well, then you need to find out who he is so they can check *him*."

"That's what I'm trying to do," I said, focusing my denial on the phone book.

"Well, good!" said Syleste, storming into the bedroom.

"And make sure you have the results before you get back into bed with me," she added softly, popping out again for a moment.

This was not the first time I had taken Sylestine's reality checks as a sign of selfishness and utter lack of faith.

I took a long look at the cut on my finger and envisioned the conversation with my friend from the intersection: "Hi. How ya doin? Good to see ya. Listen, uh . . . have you been tested for HIV lately? I was just wondering. You see my wife has exiled me to the couch until I present her with the results of *your* HIV test." Or maybe, I thought, I could just be real discreet and talk to the doctors: "You didn't happen to give this guy an HIV test, did ya doc?"

I buried these scenarios quickly, called

a few more hospital emergency rooms and asked the same question I had been asking for over an hour: "Have you admitted an Asian man in his mid-thirties with severe facial lacerations?" The responses were the same: lots of folks had been admitted with injuries caused by the violence but no Asian males in their mid-thirties with unrecognizable faces.

"I'm going over to Daniel Freeman," I announced to Syleste as I washed the blood from my hands and arms. I had been sitting in the living room calling hospitals and watching news reports for nearly an hour and a half with my friend's blood still on me. Daniel Freeman Hospital was just around the corner from our house. The news reports had said that Reginald Denny and several other victims had been taken there for treatment. I had called earlier but I thought that maybe with so many injured, they had simply misplaced my friend in a hallway somewhere.

Syleste's eyes widened. She asked me whether I was going back to Florence and Normandie.

"No. Huh-uh. Just over to the hospital

. . . to see if he's there."

As I was about to walk out the door Syleste handed me the telephone. It was my mother calling from Des Moines.

"Syleste says you're going back over there."

"No, Mom. Just over to Daniel Freeman Hospital."

"Where's that?"

"Around the corner," I assured her, narrowing my eyes at Sylestine for enlisting my mother's support. I realized then that my wife's sojourns into the bedroom that evening had probably involved conversations on the other line with my parent.

"Do you think that's wise?" Mother asked.

"It'll be okay," I said.

I promised my mother that after my trip to Daniel Freeman, I would stay in for the rest of the evening.

I left for the hospital muttering my usual playful grumbling accusations about Sylestine and Mother being in "cahoots." This was not the first time their clandestine conversations had resulted in concerned inquiries from the old homestead back in Iowa.

When I arrived at Daniel Freeman, I asked a security guard about the huge gravel truck parked in the lot. "Yeah, that's Denny's truck," he replied.

"How's he doin?" I asked.

"Still in surgery. Ain't no tellin. He's pretty messed up." The guard shook his head. "They got him here just in time. Yep, doctors said another minute and he'd a been through." It was of course five black folks who had taken Denny to the hospital that day in his truck.

The emergency room at Daniel Freeman was full of bruised and injured people waiting for treatment. Behind the thick greenish glass that separated them from the patients, the admitting staff was busily taking names and insurance cards.

Through the glass and the large locked door which swung open occasionally to admit patients, I caught glimpses of doctors and nurses treating the wounded in addition to their usual contingent of weekday emergencies. I asked an admitting clerk about my Asian friend. He left his seat for a while to make inquires, but returned with no information, for which he apologized.

I stepped outside the emergency room doors and lingered for a few moments thinking about what to do. It was then that I again noticed Denny's huge truck in the parking lot. That's it! I thought, the truck! The license plate!

It was about nine p.m. when I left Daniel Freeman and headed back to Florence and Normandie to find my friend's truck, the Ford Bronco. If I could get the license number I was sure I could find out who and possibly where he was.

Fifteen minutes later, when I arrived at the intersection, the brown Ford Bronco was nowhere to be seen. I took twenty or thirty minutes to walk the path we had taken that day. I recalled the voices I had heard, but could remember only a few of the faces. The sidewalks were empty. Only a few dim lights shone through the drawn shades and closed curtains along Florence. After my walk I returned to the inter-section's southwest corner, leaned against a familiar light pole and watched as sight-seers slowly toured the debris-littered inter-section. Amid the shattered safety glass, half-burned upholstery stuffing and bits of clothing, lay business cards and various odd-sized bits of paper. Immediately to my right I noticed a dirty bright orange overnight bag crumpled next to the curb.

I picked it up and wiped away some of the dirt and oil which obscured the name tag sewn to its side. Instantly I recognized the name written neatly on the tag: Reginald Denny, the truck driver who had been the first victim of the day. In that same instant it occurred to me that the paper and other debris in the intersection probably belonged to all the victims of the day's violence. With the next north-south red light, I walked into the street and began sorting through the documents scattered on the pavement. As the Normandie traffic resumed, I reached for several papers folded to letter size. It was a vehicle-service warranty for a brown Ford Bronco. The owner's name was Takao Hirata, and there was a phone number. I went to a pay phone on the southwest corner and called.

The woman who answered the phone explained in a pronounced Japanese accent that she was Hirata's mother and that she had been on the phone with her daughter-in-law most of the evening. Neither of them had seen or heard from Takao since early afternoon. I explained what had happened and she moaned and spoke in Japanese, her words flowing into my ears in the universal language of sorrow. She gave me her son's phone number.

I dialed the number quickly. Takao's wife, Missy, answered. I told her what had happened and she screamed once. Immediately afterward, her fright turned to determination and the two of us went about the business of finding her husband.

Police cars and shiny red trucks raced past in the fiery darkness as I drove to the emergency police command post in the Transit Authority terminal three or four miles west of Normandie. Several remote news vans were parked outside the terminal when I arrived and news reporters from the various network affiliates were doing live interviews with officers and civilians on the scene. LAPD cruisers carrying three to four officers in riot gear rolled out of the terminal in a steady stream rushing to regain the control they had relinquished earlier in the day.

I told an officer at the entrance that I could identify one of the day's victims, that his family had gone without word from him for several hours and that I believed him to be in a hospital somewhere in the area. The officer was polite but distracted. He was focusing on getting vehicles and officers in and out of the command center. I showed him the orange bag and tried to explain that it belonged to the truck driver who had been beaten that day, and that it had led me to documents that identified my friend and other victims of the violence. The officer was unable to divide his attention and, because of the day's events, my patience with peace officers was extremely thin.

I moved on to a radio reporter from KNX News Radio. I showed him the bag and told him my story. I explained that I was trying to find the man I had helped that day. The radio reporter asked if I would speak to him on the air. "Yes," I said. "And perhaps you can put his name and description out over the radio. Someone may recognize his name or his features and tell his family where he is."

One of the reporters for a local TV affiliate overheard my conversation with the radio reporter and asked if I would speak to him, live. This request came twice more from two other stations. As I would learn later, those interviews were fed directly to the networks and were being seen by folks across the country, including my parent back in Des Moines.

In each interview I recounted the day's events as I had lived them, holding up Reginald Denny's orange bag as evidence of my experience. I prefaced each interview with a request that the reporter put the word out about Takao Hirata, a name, a description. In their pursuit of the people's right to know, however, the journalists made little effort to let Takao Hirata's family know where he was or the extent of his injuries.

I returned home some time after eleven p.m. Mother was on the phone with Sylestine.

"So, you went back out there," my mother said calmly.

"Had to," I replied. "How'd you know?"

"It's all over the TV. They're calling you the Good Samaritan."

"Not in this house," I laughed, looking at my wife.

Until well after midnight, I helped Missy Hirata call medical facilities. I went to bed around two in the morning, but I could not sleep. At three a.m. someone from the Los Angeles Police Department called my home asking if I had information about the whereabouts of a missing person named Takao Hirata. I told him what I knew, and went on tossing and turning until, an hour later, Missy Hirata phoned to tell me that she had found her husband in the Metropolitan Medical Center in downtown Los Angeles.

Our early morning conversation was brief. I wished Mrs Hirata well, and asked her to give my regards to her husband.

Sylest had awakened with the ringing of the telephone, and after I hung up, I told her the good news. She gave me one of her looks, shook her head, then turned over and went to sleep.

"Well, why not?" I thought as I settled

back under the covers; the mission was accomplished. It was time to get some sleep.

Andrea: Unhappy the land that has no heroes!...
Galileo: No.   Unhappy the land that needs heroes.

BERTOLT BRECHT

LIFE OF GALILEO

8.
THREE ENCOUNTERS

The little boy, dressed in perfectly color-coordinated shirt and pants, slipped inside the door of his parents' home just as I arrived. As I stood at the bottom of the concrete steps, Missy Hirata's smile put me at ease. Inside the house, a Japanese mother welcomed me with a slight bow. A beloved brother, a high school friend, and other family members stood across the room in front of a dining table piled high with Kentucky Fried Chicken delicacies. The little boy who had ducked inside upon my arrival, the Hiratas' three-year-old son Brad, clung shyly to his mother's leg. A few feet away a short man, his face swollen and disfigured, pulled himself painfully to his feet. I stepped forward to help steady him and found myself face to face with feelings I had barricaded myself against for days. Since our meeting at that intersection I had embraced anger, self-righteousness, and doubt. But now, as I embraced my friend, the barricades crumbled and I surrendered to my tears. I could not stop thinking that Tak might have died if it had not been for the brother in the "doo rag"—and I had almost prevented him from taking Tak to the hospital because I had stereotyped him. It was not the first time I had stereotyped someone.

The man I feared above all others in the Marines was a stocky, small-eyed Drill Instructor from deepest darkest Alabama, named Sergeant Doran. He was my nemesis, who glared at me with disgust whenever he passed me. There were many days during my thirteen weeks of recruit training when I was certain I would die at the hands of this Vietnam veteran artilleryman who, to me, looked and sounded as if he could have been the Grand Dragon of the Ku Klux Klan.

Once, in the wee hours of the morning, I woke to hear Sergeant Doran's hoarse and twangy voice speaking softly just inches from my ear. I did not dare to move or even open my eyes while I listened to his frightening words. I could not see his face but I clearly envisaged his pale, pockmarked mug emitting the colorful, unthinkable torments in store for me. There was Drill Instructor Sergeant Doran, happily wiping the sweat, like blood, from his sun-baked candy apple neck . . . Drill Instructor Sergeant Doran laughing while I crawled back and forth through a foot and a half of sand under barbed wire while M-60 machine guns blazed over my head . . . Drill Instructor Sergeant Doran supervising while I, using a spoon, repeatedly buried, exhumed and identified the sex of innocent sand fleas which, according to the Sergeant, I had selfishly murdered when their only crime was a natural need to feed on my flesh.

At the end of graduation ceremonies, I hurried to get my sea bag, anticipating ten days' leave at home. My belongings stood along with my fellow Marines' gear on the concrete below our barracks. Earlier that morning platoon 2073 had vacated its home of ninety days to make room for the eighty new recruits who were due to arrive that afternoon. I shook a few hands, said a few goodbyes and see-ya-laters, and headed for the bus that would take us to the airport.

En route to the bus I spotted Sergeant Doran moving toward me at the urgent, menacing clip that was one of his dreaded characteristics. I reminded myself that I was no longer a raw recruit, but a full-fledged Marine and a Private First Class to boot. And though the Sergeant still out-ranked me, this time I was prepared to make a stand. In fact, I thought to myself, while I trembled, I might even dare to toss a few choice words in the approximate direction of the good Sergeant from Ala-bama! I steeled myself as he approached, gritting my teeth.

He smiled at me and held out his hand.

"Private First Class Williams, congratula-tions. I'm real proud of ya, Marine," he said.

It seemed like an eternity before I was able to raise my hand to his. I was confused and shaken, to say the least. For nearly three months I had considered this man to be my enemy, only in part because of his intimidat-ing words and ugly threats which were often realized. I know now that, unlike my reaction to the other drill instructors, I had considered Sergeant Doran to be my enemy from the very beginning. I know now that his Southern origin, his accent, his features and his manner had combined to prevent me from seeing any possibility that the Sergeant might simply be a man who was teaching me how to stay alive, to go the extra mile, not to quit no matter what happened. That he was a guy doing what he had been trained to do, the best way he knew how to do it.

On the one hand, Sergeant Doran may well have owned a closet full of white sheets and hoods. And then, on the other hand, a man may not always be what he appears on the surface to be.

We shook hands, Sergeant Doran and I. He wished me well and strode off as quickly as he had come, heading toward his next bunch of would-be warriors. I felt no affection for him in 1974 and even now, twenty years later, my memories of him are not particularly fond. Nevertheless, when I do remember that son of Alabama, I think of how perceptions molded by stereotyping can cultivate fear, and poison all hope of understanding.

When I was a teenager, my father figure Mr Bus occasionally called me a knucklehead. I hung my head in shame when he called me that, because I knew it meant that whatever I had done was as stupid as it was wrong. Usually I earned that name when I did things that were not only selfish but self-destructive. When Mr Bus called me a knucklehead, I knew that he wanted me to wake—to wise up and look reality straight in the eye.

A knucklehead is a hardhead: all bone above the shoulders. No eyes to see where he's headed. No nose to smell his own bull. No ears to hear the lies others tell him, the lies he tells himself.

In June of 1993 I travelled to Iowa, back to Des Moines to salvage what was left of years of living, after the so-called Great Flood of '93 had ravaged my mother's basement. When things more or less returned to normal after ten days or so of no water for baths and no air-conditioning, I kissed Mother and Grandmother goodbye and headed up to Minnesota to see my publicist Zoé Diacou, before returning to Los Angeles. We were on the way to an appointment when Zoé stopped at one of my favorite places—a Kinko's. As she pulled into a parking stall near the entrance, two men—one in his early twenties, the other around thirty-five—came out of the copy center. The older man wore a tattered leather jacket; the other was dressed in a faded green military field coat. Their heads were close shaven; only stubble remained. "They look like skinheads," I remarked, as Zoé turned off the ignition.

Smiling, she agreed that they certainly had that look.

As I stepped out of the car, I caught the young one's eye. He paused, reached into his pocket, pulled out a piece of paper and, without taking his eyes from mine, gave it a long lick. Then he turned and slammed the paper against the stucco wall where it remained, too far for my nearsighted eyes to read it. The older fellow had kept walking toward their car which was parked parallel to us, about twenty-five or thirty feet away. While the younger man went to the driver's side of his car, I walked over to the wall to see what he had put up there. "WHITE POWER" it said, and something about saving the white race. A swastika appeared behind the words, and at the bottom of the sheet was an address where the interested could send for information. Quickly I swung around, and faced the two men who were just opening the doors of their car.

"Oh, ya'll skinheads?" I said, with a grin. "Ya'll are like—Nazis, right?"

They grinned back at me and nodded. I began to laugh.

"So you guys are part of the master race? You two?" I pointed at them in disbelief and roared with laughter. They were ragged and pale, with dark circles under their eyes. They certainly looked nothing like the blond, blue-eyed endangered species they were trying to save from extinction. "Ya'll don't like niggers, right?"

"You got it," one said.

"Okay, cool. Here's a nigger. Kill him!" I raised my voice. "Here's one lone nigger, and there's two of you. If you kill me now there'll be one less nigger to worry about, right?" I was raving; I think I heard Zoé saying something about going inside.

The younger one shifted from side to side and clenched his fists. He looked as though he wanted to make a move—as though he was chomping at the bit for a personal taste of the second "final solution." But, instead, he decided to join his partner who was already sitting in the car. Although they were visibly disturbed by my attempt to challenge their agenda, by the time their old engine ignited and their battered car began backing out of the stall, they were both smiling confidently. I didn't get the impression that either of them was frightened. I think they had simply decided to bide their time. On the other hand I, like so many other folks, had stopped biding my time some years before: in the matter of paranoid hatemongers with low self-esteem, the best defense, I have come to believe, is a good offense—'cause like the song says, "I've come too far to turn around now." Never again.

While they were driving out of the parking lot, the pair saw me remove the paper from the wall and put it in my pocket. I had every intention of sending for my portion of their insightful literature.

If Mr Bus had been there that day he would have stood watching quietly, with his hand closed protectively over his left rear pocket. Then afterward he would have slapped me on the back of my skull and called me a knucklehead. Slapped me— but not so hard that I'd think he didn't love me. And he would have been fully justified. That had been a very knucklehead thing to do—an example of downright stupidity fueled by an old rage that can rise boiling hot in the space of a heartbeat.

The deception of others is usually rooted in the deception of one's self.

BILL WILSON
AS BILL SEES IT

9.
WOLVES WITHIN

By the second day of the Los Angeles Riots, I was absolutely livid with rage. I had witnessed firsthand, close up, live and in dying color, the consequences of intolerance and unchecked anger. Yet folks were running around screaming about uprisings and revolutions—seemingly unable or unwilling to make distinctions between legitimate protests against systemic injustice, and terrorism.

At first glance, in the wake of the verdict, the gathering of African Americans at the corner of Florence and Normandie was reminiscent of an earlier time—an exciting, liberating time: "nation time." It had been too long since black folks had seen black folks on television coming together in America to proclaim their worth, instead of mourning the pointless drowning of another father, mother or child in a dead concrete sea of despair.

Consequently many sailed to the scene in proud protest and then scuttled the vessel by ignoring the ships that were sinking all around them—ignoring the cries for help as perhaps these indifferent sailors' own fathers and grandfathers and great-grandfathers had been ignored as they cried out while they were being dragged to the hanging tree and the stake. "If I am only for myself . . . what am I?"

Thus some of us just watched and some even cheered while knuckleheads beat the living daylights out of the innocent. "If not now . . . when?"

In the first few days after the "unrest" I was extremely angry; during interviews with the media I referred to individuals—specifically African Americans—who appeared to have committed acts of violence, as knuckleheads. Most of the time I tried to be sure to add that I myself had acted like a knucklehead on more than one occasion. "Still do, sometimes," I said. I called those sad dark brothers and sisters knuckleheads because it takes one to know one. I only hope now that I didn't slap them so hard or say it so loud that they would think I didn't love them.

Since that Spring of 1992, a number of apparently well-intentioned folks have tried to rationalize senseless acts of violence. These rationalizations were offered by the counterparts of those who, after the beating of Rodney King, sought to justify the savagery of men sworn to represent and uphold the law.

A reporter for a national newspaper was sitting beside me at an international conference on children and violence. "Those officers were doing their duty," she said. I told her that I thought that the Rodney King beating bore the same stamp of mob brutality as the savagery at the corner of Florence and Normandie. Her response made no bones about how she felt: she said that she believed that the violence at that intersection was perpetrated by criminals and thugs. I agreed. But what about Rodney King?

She gathered up her things. "The officers accused of beating Mr King were sworn uni-

formed officials of the state," she said, and
hurried to the door.

So, I thought, were the Gestapo. I was
saddened and surprised by the forgetfulness
of this daughter of German Jewish refugees.

Many people clearly thought that Law-
rence Powell and Stacey Koon and the other
policemen were really protecting us in a
reasonable way from dangerous black bully
boys whose own threatening behavior—even
when they were prostrate on the ground—
had contributed to their bashings. Even
after hundreds of years, an old style of injustice exists for dark young men: their
unshackled maleness still incites brutality
in those who are insecure about their own
masculinity.

And then, one year later, many of us who
had cried foul at that first beating, used the
very real and reeking record of old injus-
tices, if not to justify, then at the very least
to excuse, the robbery and beating of men
and women whose prostrate, bloody forms
received the same cowardly kicks and blows
which had been visited upon their darker
brothers.

In the wake of the riot, so-called liberals

and self-styled civil rights professionals began to scramble for network sound bites.
New Hueys and Bobbys and Eldridges, who
had long ago traded their berets for business
suits and their naturals for no-lye relaxers,
literally rose from the ashes, flaming with
prophetic rhetoric which their handlers assured them reflected the politically correct
view of a city in partial ruin. Liberal guilt was
now revived and victim status reasserted: the
call went out for money, jobs and housing.
These were the things, the liberals and self-
styled leaders said, that would fix what had
gone wrong.

There is no question, of course, that the
disproportionate distribution of wealth and
opportunity in this nation has contributed
and continues to contribute to the climate of
despair which exists in many communities
of color. Indispensable components for
the rebuilding of the individual, and there-
by the community, are employment at a
living wage, funds for education and the
construction and renovation of decent af-
fordable housing. But somehow jobs, education and housing seem superficial in the
light of the emotional and psychological

trauma inflicted upon generations of African people in America, in the light of the handing down of that trauma from one generation to the next, and in the light of the contemporary handiwork of those who profit from selling young black children the sole status of victim. One might consider jobs, education and housing to be an inadequate solution when one thinks about the things that were going on in the hearts and heads of the African Americans who demonstrated such dysfunctional brutal behavior as that which was seen at the intersection of Florence and Normandie avenues on April 29, 1992. And that behavior, not televised, is a daily occurrence tolerated in communities across America.

The violence witnessed at that intersection is par for the daily obstacle course for millions of people, both old and young. How can one focus on an excellent performance at a good job when one spends the entire day worrying about the safety of those whom one is laboring to provide for? What bearing does a solid education have on the trajectory of a gangster's bullet? Where is the gain in affirmative action and equal access to opportunity if the terror wreaked by "new" night riders condemns us to hide behind the barred windows of our besieged homes? Our hard-won gains might get us temporarily out of harm's way in some isolated suburb; perhaps some of us can sleep in peace while the community we left behind is devoured by wolves both without and within.

We have met the enemy and they is us.

POGO

 10.
AN INSIDE JOB

In July of 1992 I made the mistake of suggesting on national television that a significant portion of what needed fixing in some black communities might be an inside job.

I had turned down several invitations to appear on talk shows because I was afraid of a political, exploitive approach. But the people from the Phil Donahue show assured me that the format would not be confrontational. "We've done that already," the producer said on the phone. "This show will be about victims of the violence and the people who helped."

That sounded good. And Sylestine and I were due to be in Washington, D.C. a few days before the date of the Donahue show. A day or two in New York sounded like fun.

So I accepted the invitation.

On the morning of the show, outside the Drake Hotel, I shook hands with two young African-American men. We were all waiting for transportation to the studio. I assumed these two were victims of the riots or were people who had helped somebody. Just before the car arrived to pick us up, Bobby Green joined us. Sylest and I had met him the previous evening; he was one of the five people who had come to the aid of Reginald Denny. When the car pulled up, the driver said that he was supposed to take Sylest, Mr Green and me to the studio. He said another car would be along soon to pick up the other two young men. I didn't think much about this at the time.

At the studio, Sylest, Mr Green and I shared a dressing room with two Korean-Americans: Jay Rhee, a merchant who had been guarding his business with a gun, and Angela Oh, a lawyer and spokeswoman for the L.A. Korean community. Mr Donahue dropped in for a visit fifteen or twenty minutes before the show was to begin. He gave us a pep talk, told us not to be nervous and assured us that he was deeply interested in helping to heal the wounds of Los Angeles.

We were marched out onto the set a few minutes before show time and assigned our seats. As the sound technicians were adjusting our microphones, the two young men entered whom I had met outside the Drake Hotel. Jim Brown, the athlete-actor-activist was with them. These three African-American men were seated at one end of the platform. I was placed at the opposite end. Between us the director seated the two Korean Americans. Bobby Green was given a chair in the audience.

I didn't like the look of this seating arrangement at all. I began to suspect that something was terribly wrong here. When the show began, Phil introduced the two young African-American men as former rival gang members who were working with Jim Brown to secure peace on the streets: one was called Bone and the other Little Monster. I realized that the format of this show was going to be different from what I had been led to expect it would be.

Once I grasped what the producers of this show had in mind, I began talking to myself in silent urgency. Be cool, Gregory,

I said to myself. Just relax. I took this advice for about five minutes. But I lost my cool when Bone said that the "whole riot thing" had been about class struggle. If that's the case, I thought to myself, then why was the proletariat beating up the peasants and not the damn decadent bourgeoisie?

So I began to talk—maybe I was strident and confrontational—and I called Mr Hirata's assailants thugs, murderers and thieves. I demanded to know why, when an African-American life was threatened or snuffed out by a white person, all hell broke loose. But when an African-American gunslinger killed his African-American rival—or worse, an innocent African-American child—why were there no marches, no protests, no cries of outrage? While the black panel members assailed the wickedness of the system, I wondered out loud about the sheep within the flock who behaved like wolves—those younger members of the flock who were devouring other young lambs on their way to the rich grassland of the American dream.

At the top of the first commercial break,

Little Monster asked me, with a sneer, "Yo, brother, where you from?"

Here we go, I said to myself. "Iowa, Des Moines, born and raised," I announced. I knew what was coming next.

"Oh, okay," he said, smiling. "I see where you're comin from."

This wasn't the first time that my views on self-appraisal and self-healing had been denigrated because I was a native of Iowa—a state which is certainly not noted for its large black population. In fact, most people I meet—black and white—respond to my telling them where I'm from by saying something like, "Really? I didn't know there were black people in Iowa."

Sometimes I tell people that my mother took the train north from Mississippi and got off at Des Moines because she thought the conductor said it was Detroit. The truth, however, is that African Americans have been in Iowa since at least the early nineteenth century. They have been farmers, miners, lawyers, teachers, scientists, and builders of entire towns. But, sadly, lots of folks have come to accept the big city ghetto and/or the cotton belt as the geographical be-all and end-all of the African-American experience.

I had planned to avoid public discussion about my actions during the riot: I did not want to diminish the good will engendered by what I had done, with talk about my personal opinions. When I look at the tape of that Donahue show today, it is all too clear that I was angry and frustrated by this politicalization of the violence at the corner of Florence and Normandie. I was aware at the time that my view of events was not the one that was being aired on television every night. I knew there was, in some circles at least, to be little discussion of any issue except victimization. The disappointing fact is that of all the media, both serious and frivolous, which seemed to seek the truth about what happened at that intersection, absolutely no African-American media, either print or broadcast, contacted me for details of what had happened. I do not say this because I have a bruised or unfulfilled ego, but I present it as evidence of my belief that within the African-American community there was little or no desire for an open and candid public discussion of what had gone so terribly wrong that day. Over the months since, I have received dozens of congratulatory comments from black people for what was really not my doing at all. But sadly, many of these congratulations were delivered in whispers. Recently a new acquaintance told me over the phone that he was happy about my helping Mr Hirata because it showed "them" that "we aren't all like that."

I thought, For God's sake, who cares what "they" think? I didn't help that man so that I could be considered a credit to my race; I did it simply because it was the right thing to do. I've heard lots of friendly comments like that, and they serve to reinforce my belief that we still have to shake off the yoke of a desire for the approval of our former masters.

But to return to the Donahue show. Having assured themselves that I was a brainwashed reactionary Negro, Bone and Little Monster, abetted by Jim Brown, began to bait me with a bit more confidence. Little Monster said that he and Bone had been in jail, but now that they were out, they had been working in the community. "Ask Greg where he's been," Little Monster said.

Jim Brown said that I was a hero because the camera caught my act. He implied that my being on the Donahue show was the "commercialization of a hero." I found this remark very sad, coming from a man whose athletic prowess had brought him much commercial success. I hadn't received one dime for doing what I was supposed to do anyhow.

The two Korean Americans were brought into the heated discussion and accused, by implication, of having a destructive effect on the black community because, among other things, they owned liquor stores there. I said I wanted to talk about solutions for the serious problem of addiction in the community; I didn't want to talk about who was responsible for the addiction. I didn't want to blame white people or Koreans: rather, I said, than mourn the loss of vital young black lives, we should tell these young people that they play a role in their own destinies.

Donahue, saying he was impressed with the "passion" I brought to this dialogue, jumped up on the stage, crouched down beside me and whispered loudly into my ear and into the microphone, that it would probably embarrass me to know that I would get a standing ovation at most white Rotary clubs for what I had said. It certainly wasn't what Black America wanted to hear.

The activists down front applauded wildly. They obviously did not understand that their host had just suggested that only white folks give a hoot about teaching their kids the importance of personal responsibility and self-discipline.

I was carried away by emotion and—regrettably—I used the tragic and needless death of young Latasha Harlins as an example of what I was talking about. "When Latasha Harlins walked into that store," I said, "she had control over her life, but because of her actions, she lost it." Whether that woman had killed her out of frustration, fear or anger, I said, Latasha Harlins could have prevented her own death. If a knucklehead is swinging a baseball bat and I step in front of him, don't I share responsibility for my injuries?

Even as I was speaking these words, I

knew I had crossed the line. And when the contingent of black activists seated in the front in the audience began to boo and heckle me, I was certain of it. If I could have called back those words, I would have done it at once. Good old Phil, sensing a ratings opportunity, shouted, "You're not going to get very far blaming Latasha for her own death!"

In all the commotion, I said I was trying to make a statement about taking control of what goes on in the black community. But Phil said again that I was trying to blame the victim.

"That's not what I'm saying," I said, "and you know very well that's not what I'm saying, Mr Donahue."

"Are you saying," Donahue yelled, "that when she turned around to walk out of that store she should have known she was going to get a bullet in the head?"

The audience was certainly wildly against me. I tried to say that what I meant was that children must be taught that when they do inappropriate things they put themselves in danger. But I was in shock for the next several minutes. I was embarrassed and humiliated; I had been set up by a sideshow smoothy with a perm.

Ultimately, the conversation had come down to accountability. Certainly I was not trying to imply that if Ms Harlins had attempted to steal a bottle of orange juice from the grocery store it warranted the theft of her life. In fact, I believe the punishment for her alleged "crime" was tantamount to a lynching. And the sentence of "probation" given Latasha's murderer raises serious questions about the judicial view of the value of an African-American life. But, if she did indeed attempt to steal, hadn't her actions placed her in jeopardy?

Undoubtedly there are all sorts of knuckleheads out there: racist Nazis, greedy gangsters, uninformed officials and angry paranoid grocers with hair-trigger magnums. If I am to be anything other than fodder for their bloody agendas, I must keep my head up, my eyes open and do all I can to stay out of range of their weapons. At the very least I reduce the odds that I will fall victim to their insanity.

During the penultimate commercial break I apologized to the brothers on the panel for having allowed myself to be used. I wasn't apologizing for my opinions, but for having been made an unwitting accomplice in what seemed to me to be a deliberate manipulation—pitting black man against black man for the sake of ratings and advertising revenue. My apology was accepted.

Before the last commercial I let Phil know that I knew what was going on and I didn't like it. I didn't like the fact that I had allowed him to pit me against other black men. That happened all the time, I said.

"Your objection is duly noted," he said, and moved away from me.

I said that actually the brothers and I had the same goals. And I apologized to them once more.

And in fact I believe our goals *are* the same: to find and implement solutions to the genocidal behavior that claims far too many African-American lives. We differed only on the question of approach, focus and perhaps personal experience. Little Monster, Bone, Jim Brown and I are not enemies. In fact, Jim Brown had been a hero to me at a time when black actors first started winning heroic roles. Each time I saw Jim Brown dodging the bad guy's bullets, riding tall in the saddle on a par with his white counterparts, I felt more hope and pride than one can imagine—unless one is a somewhat insecure young brown boy, who dreams silver-screen dreams.

Sylestine had watched the show from the green room, and she tried to soothe me when I entered, but I was, as Mother used to say, "hoppin mad."

I asked Sylest to get our things together; I wanted to leave as soon as possible. I had served my purpose, and the producers and production assistants, who had been so gracious before the show, now had little or nothing to say to us. But before they could hustle out the used camera fodder, I paid a visit to the dressing room on the other side of the hall where the producers had sequestered the fox from the hounds or the hounds from the fox, depending on one's point of view.

We shook hands and exchanged a few polite words. The black female producer who had brought the brothers to the show was standing there; she smiled at them and assured them that they had done a wonderful job. As I left the room, she came after me, pulled the door closed behind her and glanced down the hallway in both directions before she looked me in the eye and said, "You made some valid points, but there's just some things you shouldn't say in front of white folks."

Whoops! There, I've done it again!

There is plenty of courage among us for the abstract but not for the concrete.

HELEN KELLER
LET US HAVE FAITH

11.
EVIDENCE OF INHUMANITY

More than a year later I was called to testify at the trial of the two men charged with beating Reginald Denny, Takao Hirata and others. When I arrived at the witness waiting room of the Los Angeles County Criminal courts building I found Tak was sitting with another man; they were both reading the LA *Times*. Tak smiled broadly when he saw me; he stood up and we hugged each other. The second man introduced himself and shook my hand firmly. He was an unheralded hero named Jorge Gonzalez. This was our second meeting: the last time he had extended his hand to me, he had been knocked off his feet by a violent blow to the face.

Some months before our meeting I had learned that as I pulled Mr Hirata from his vehicle, Jorge had left his own car and made

his way to my side. Just as the brave young
Mexican-American man was reaching out for
Tak and me, he had been struck. He had
stumbled backward and was set upon by
several cowards who gleefully kicked and
beat him as he lay in the streets. He managed to drag himself to his feet during a
momentary lull in the savagery, but then
was knocked to the ground again. I believe
that Mr Gonzalez took the blows which were
meant for me that day—because, in fact,
Jorge's courage and compassion created a
diversion which drew the attackers' focus
away from Mr Hirata and me. I thank God
that among the heroes who gathered for me
on that day was one brave and beloved Jorge
Gonzalez.

Tak, Jorge and I spent most of the
brief time while we were waiting to testify,
joking about our experiences at Florence
and Normandie. But there were moments
too when the bitter consequences of that
day's violence burst through the veneer of
laughter. Jorge was a third-year law student
at the University of Southern California. His
voice became soft, his eyes lowered and dis-
tant when he spoke of being so badly beaten

that he could hardly make it through his law school finals. By getting out of his car to help Tak and me, he had literally laid years of purposeful labor on the line and nearly lost everything.

I told Tak and Jorge about my clarinet, and how since our first meeting I had come to understand something of the theft that occurs when violence is done. Tak nodded silently and said that he understood.

"I'm okay," he said softly, without smiling. "But then I don't remember anything."

"Neither do I," said Jorge.

"That's probably a blessing." Tak laughed.

"Yeah," Jorge muttered. "Probably."

Tak was called to the witness stand first. Then I was called. I grabbed my jacket and shook hands with Jorge. I assured him I would call. I put on my jacket, straightened my tie and headed towards the courtroom.

When I was on the stand the defense attorney Wilma Shanks asked me, in an accusatory tone, why I had kept Reginald Denny's orange overnight bag for such a long time. I tried to explain that it was only the week before I was scheduled to testify that the attorneys for the prosecution had learned that I had the bag.

At about seven o'clock on a Monday evening in the District Attorney's office, while we were reviewing my upcoming testimony, I happened to mention finding the bag and that its discovery had led me to Takao's vehicle service warranty.

The prosecutor Janet Moore popped upright in her chair and asked in unison with her two colleagues, "Bag? What bag?"

She asked me to describe the overnight bag, and then invited me to step across the hall with her to a room with a video tape machine. Within moments I was watching a black man jump from the cab of a large truck clutching a small orange overnight bag in his hand. "Is that the bag, Mr Williams?"

"Yes, that's the bag," I replied; I realized then for the first time that evidence in a criminal trial had been sitting in a storage container above my parking space at home for more than a year.

"Didn't you know," Ms Shanks said, "that my client Damion Williams has been charged with the burglary of Mr Denny's bag?"

"No, I didn't."

"Why did you keep evidence sitting in your living room?" Her attitude was challenging.

"I didn't see it as evidence in any legal sense," I explained. "If it was evidence of anything, I saw it as evidence of inhumanity."

At one point in my testimony I referred to the bag as "emotional" memorabilia. Just fifteen minutes after I had left the witness stand, while the D.A. investigators were driving me to work, the local news station broadcast a teaser promoting their upcoming newscast which would feature a TV actor who had withheld evidence for over a year. With excited disbelief the announcer proclaimed, ". . . and after helping a victim of the riots, the TV actor went back to the intersection to search for souvenirs."

Boy, did that hurt!

Since the day of our first reunion, Takao and I have talked only a few times. Although I've been tested for HIV a couple of times since we met, I've never talked to Tak about it. A while back he gave me a wonderful miniature samurai helmet. "You are my samurai," he said. I was so proud and honored, all I could say was, "Wow!"

I've been on the road working a lot lately, and Takao and his family are slowly and successfully rebuilding their lives. Tak and I have promised ourselves that, no matter what, one day, we're going bowling.

In the congratulatory wake of my good deed I am compelled to ask myself, am I hero or penitent? Today, my Japanese-American friend insists that he owes me a debt. I hope that one day he will understand that what I gave him was simply payment of a debt long overdue.

Justice is like a train that's nearly always late.

YEVGENY YEVTUSHENKO
A PRECOCIOUS AUTOBIOGRAPHY

12.
IN SEARCH OF JUSTICE

One afternoon more than three months after the riot, when the city was beginning its long and difficult rehabilitation, Detective Chase of the Los Angeles Police Department appeared at my door. He was the first law enforcement official I had spoken to since the incident. I invited him in, he took a seat on the sofa and presented me with several notebooks which contained photos of young men and women who had been identified as having gang affiliations. Detective Chase suggested that among the photos I might recognize some of those who had participated in the beating of Mr Hirata.

Each group of photos was cataloged by gang name. Some had even been broken down by neighborhood and street. I searched each volume thoroughly, but the only face I recognized was my own. In the second notebook I found a picture of a teenager who bore a striking resemblance to a snapshot of myself at fifteen or so.   I asked the detective about that young man, but he could not give me any specifics; he only said with confidence that neither that boy nor any of the others in the notebooks were worth the paper their images had been printed on. Smiling, Detective Chase assured me that the boy who looked like me and all the others who had found their way into his notebook files were animals hopelessly beyond redemption.

I finished the obligatory viewing feeling profoundly sad, but also relieved that I could now show the police officer, and his opinions, politely to the door.

And what about the young men who committed acts of brutality on that day? Was there no one to teach them? When they were growing into the monsters that we have labeled them, were there no heroes to save them from themselves? I am grateful to have been there for my friend, Tak Hirata, but perhaps we all should have been at that intersection long before that tragic day in April. If I had been there then, how many might have been spared a coarse and bitter fate? How many might have been rescued, or can yet be rescued, if there were only a gathering of heroes?